THE CAREER CONNECTION FOR TECHNICAL EDUCATION

A Guide to Technical Training and Related Career Opportunities

Second Edition

Fred A. Rowe, Ed. D.

SECOND EDITION

The Career Connection for Technical Education—*A Guide to Technical Training and Related Career Opportunities*

JIST Works, Inc.
720 North Park Avenue
Indianapolis, IN 46202–3431
1-317-264-3720 • Fax: 1-317-264-3709

The Career Connection for College Education
Another book by Dr. Rowe that uses a format similar to this book,
but is designed for those considering four-year college majors. Price: $16.95,
ISBN: 1-56370-142-1.

Other Titles: JIST publishes a variety of career reference books on job seeking and
career information.
Order Information: See the last page of this book for an order form or contact us
for additional information. Qualified schools and institutions may request our
catalog of more than 500 career-related books, videos, and software.
Errors and omissions: We have been careful to provide accurate information throughout this
book, but it is possible that errors have been inadvertently introduced. Please consider this
in making any career plans or other important decisions. Trust your own judgment above all
else and in all things.

Library of Congress Cataloging-In-Publications Data

Rowe, Fred A.
    The career connection for technical education : a guide to
technical education and related career opportunities / Fred A. Rowe.
— 2nd ed.
      p.   cm.
    Includes index.
    ISBN 1-56370-143-X
    1. Technology—Vocational guidance—United States—Handbooks,
manuals, etc.   2. Industrial arts—Vocational guidance—United
States—Handbooks, manuals, etc.   3. Technical education—United
States—Handbooks, manuals, etc.   I. Title.
T65.3.R69   1994
602.3'73—dc20   94-16434
                                         CIP

ISBN: 1-56370-143-X

Table of Contents

This section describes more than 60 technical majors including: Description • Emphases Within Each Major • Typical College Courses • Related High School Courses • Related Careers With Beginning Salaries and Outlook • Related Occupational Personality Styles • Data, People, Things Level of Functioning • GOE Work Groups

Auxiliary Information   155

Indexes   165

The Reasons This Book Is Important to You

The fact that you are reading this book indicates your interest in the possibility of further education. That is a big decision. It affects not only what you will be doing in the short term but also the circumstances surrounding your work and your lifestyle. Education affects careers, and careers impact our lives. Families, geography, self-worth, and financial resources are all integrated so completely with our work.

For most people, the period between ages 16 and 25 is a peak time for decision making. This is when they determine educational goals, select a technical school or university, find a major, decide on a career, and begin a career path. With the increasing demands of the labor market, more and more adults also find the need to make important career, education, and training decisions. These decisions are important and require a heavy investment in both time and energy.

Because selecting a career is so vital, nearly everyone needs help with it. It is true that most students will receive career information of one kind or another: some will receive it from an important acquaintance, others will find it by chance, and many will receive structured career counseling.

Career decision making is not, as some may believe, a linear process. One usually does not first pick a college, next choose an appropriate major, and then select a career. Nor does one select a career, next choose an appropriate major, and then pick a college offering that curriculum. Many times, students will hop into the middle of the process and select a major first; or more precisely, they will enroll in courses and then see if they are happy and successful.

Selecting a technical major and narrowing the possibilities for a career can be exciting. You are the most important person in your life. The quality of your happiness, self-fulfillment, and service is dramatically influenced by how well you plan.

Although career decision making is a complex process, it becomes a lot easier if you

1. know who you are, what you can do, and what you want out of life;
2. have a pool of career and educational information; and
3. talk with knowledgeable people who can help you harmonize who you are with the educational and career alternatives that are acceptable and accessible to you.

Target Groups Helped by This Book

The Career Connection for Technical Education provides a variety of information arranged in a simple-to-use format that is useful to many types of individuals.

Students Both in high school and beyond, students need information about themselves and educational or career alternatives. The times when this book can be of most help are:
- At registration times when you have to select those courses that may be most helpful in preparing you for technical training or education
- When you have general questions about how much education you want after high school
- As you have some questions about a few careers that seem high on your list and you want to know what educational majors these are related to
- When you work with counselors, friends, and parents in registering for your first semester at a technical or vocational institution
- As you try to narrow down the possibilities of a technical major
- At those times when you are wondering what your personality and interests are and how they relate to careers

Counselors This book is a particularly valuable resource for both high school and college counselors. Its advantage over encyclopedia-type reference books are (a) its ease of reading, (b) the broad variety of information, and (c) the frequency with which students will use it. Here are some times when this book has proven to be most useful.
- At registration
- For classes in career education as a textbook—its ability to help students understand themselves, then use that self-awareness to contemplate educational and career opportunities is effective
- When helping students plan for higher education, admissions, and first enrollment
- In small group experiences with students
- With parents and students in small groups as they plan for their high school registrations and post secondary educational activities
- In vocational career classes
- In school career centers, as a valuable resource with other college catalogs

The Career Connection for Technical Education

Parents Parental involvement in their children's education is continually sought by educators and its value is unsurpassed. Simply put, families have the greatest impact on youth decisions for careers. Here are some ways you can use this book.

- To show students the relationship between careers and education
- At critical points in their high school and technical careers, such as when entering high school and in the transition from high school to a technical or vocational educational program
- When attempting to help your children understand themselves better in areas of personality types that relate to careers, how their school courses can be a barometer for technical majors, and how their interests relate to technical training and careers
- When providing information about education and careers that is hard to pick out of large encyclopedias
- As your children become lost, bored, or uneasy about the meaning of their educational experiences
- To help them look at a broader expanse of career and educational opportunities that may not have been available to you as a parent

Teachers While most classes are not thought of as career preparatory classes, their meaning can be increased to students by relating what is being learned in class to further educational and occupational realms. Here are a few ideas.

- A quick reference to careers and majors related to your classes
- A way to self-exploration
- As a guide to those students who seem lost or uncertain
- To broaden the vision of students who have gender issues related to accessible career opportunities

Career Changers and Displaced Workers This is a critical time in one's life—a time when thoughts turn to retraining. For displaced homemakers trying to be both parents, breadwinner, and student, ideas for short-term training seem applicable. For displaced workers, the emphasis to catch up on current methods, ideas, and knowledge is imperative. Here are a few ideas that can help you use this book.

- To identify who you are—this is a critical issue when disappointment has bludgeoned your self-esteem
- To see what is available on the current market and what the salaries and outlooks are
- When re-evaluating your original desires for the amount of education you wanted
- To compare the length of time and commitment needed to major in certain areas that seem acceptable to you
- To compare your personality style, interests, and the skills you already possess with related jobs and educational areas

How to Use This Book

The book has been designed to be flexible by providing several ways to approach the career exploration process. You can use the Table of Contents to quickly identify a technical major, then turn to that section in the book for more detailed information. You can also look up a specific job title in the Career Index and find its related educational requirements. Another very effective way is to identify what you are like in relation to careers and college majors. *The Career Connection for Technical Education* is divided into seven major sections.

Part One   This is the introductory section on The Reasons This Book Is Important to You.

Part Two   There are several groups of people that can benefit from *The Career Connection for Technical Education*. They are identified with various ways of utilizing the information within the book.

Part Three   The value of important information in the process of career and educational decision making is discussed.

Part Four   This section provides you an opportunity to study yourself and see how your personality and interests, along with your inclination to work with information, people, or concrete objects, relate to various college majors and work groups. It includes
1. A description of various occupational personality styles and their relationships to college majors and the *Guide for Occupational Exploration* (GOE) interest area work groups
2. A description of the various GOE work groups and their relationship to the college majors
3. Types of school courses or subjects and their relationship to the various college majors and GOE work groups
4. What functions are considered in working with data, people, or things and the college majors and GOE work groups that have "high" requirements in each of those three categories

Part Five   This section describes more than 60 technical majors, including:
1. A general description of each technical major and the type of career-related work it leads to
2. Various job titles, outlook for future openings, and starting salaries related to each major

3. A code number for each occupation that cross-references the reader to the *Dictionary of Occupational Titles*, a major career information source published by the U.S. Department of Labor
4. The types of courses typically required in each area of study
5. High school courses that best prepare for the area of study or that indicate an ability to succeed in that area
6. The occupational personality styles that are best for the major
7. Whether the major requires tasks that are high, medium, or low in the areas of working with data, people, or things
8. The general interest areas of the *Guide for Occupational Exploration* that relate to the specific major

Part Six This part includes ideas concerning
1. The relationship between levels of education and careers
2. The different types of educational opportunities after high school
3. Ideas on admissions
4. The anatomy of a job

Part Seven For easier access to the various technical majors and their related careers, two indexes are provided. The first is an alphabetical listing of the majors and their corresponding page numbers. The second index provides an alphabetical listing of nearly 1,000 careers and their corresponding page numbers. It will be noted that many careers can emerge from more than one technical major.

This variety of information is provided in a simple-to-use format that should be useful for most users. The information is general in nature and can't replace the careful review of a school's catalog of course offerings and requirements. Many schools will have specific requirements that may differ from those presented here, and the names of their major areas of study may also differ. But the information contained here is helpful in identifying areas of interest that are worthy of more consideration.

Information that resulted in the projection of beginning salaries was derived from (a) 16 specifically selected college and university placement offices, (b) national professional organizations, (c) regional manpower studies printed by the information services of Job Service, and (d) national publications including "Federal Civilian Workforce Statistics: Occupations of Federal White-Collar and Blue-Collar Workers," printed by the U.S. Office of Personnel Management; "Comparison of Annual Salaries in Private Industry with Salary Rates of Federal Employees;" and the "General Schedule: National Survey of Professional, Administrative, Technical, and Clerical Pay," printed by the U.S. Department of Labor, Bureau of Labor Statistics.

This government publication is often found in the offices of most counselors or in career centers and libraries. It provides descriptions of over 12,000 jobs and is an important reference for you to know about.

If an occupation is included in this publication, it has a reference number which is actually a code. By looking up the title, you can read a brief description about the job and environment along with some ideas of tasks used on the job.

The sample number is broken down into a working code below:

SAMPLE

005.	061	–	014
Occupational Group	Worker Functions		Alphabetical Order of Titles

OCCUPATIONAL GROUP

The first three digits classify specific occupational groups. The first digit represents nine cluster occupations, including:

0/1	Professional, Technical, and Managerial	5	Processing
2	Clerical and Sales	6	Machine Trades
3	Service	7	Benchwork
4	Agricultural, Fishing, and Forestry	8	Structural Work
		9	Miscellaneous

Degrees associated with college majors are found mostly in the 0/1 and 2 occupational group. The second two digits of the occupational code are categorized into 82 specific divisions such as engineering, education, music, etc.

WORKER FUNCTIONS

The second set of three digits identifies the types of tasks most often associated or used in the specific occupation. When working, according to this government publication, we perform specific tasks centered around DATA, PEOPLE, or THINGS. A particular occupation may emphasize each of these three categories with different intensities. The D.O.T. simply lists the major types of tasks associated with each of the three categories.

4th Digit = **Data**	5th Digit = **People**	6th Digit = **Things**
0 Synthesizing	0 Mentoring	0 Setting Up
1 Coordinating	1 Negotiating	1 Precision Working
2 Analyzing	2 Instructing	2 Operating-Controlling
3 Compiling	3 Supervising	3 Driving-Operating
4 Computing	4 Diverting	4 Manipulating
5 Copying	5 Persuading	5 Tending
6 Comparing	6 Speaking-Signaling	6 Feeding—offbearing
	7 Serving	7 Handling
	8 Taking Instructions— Helping	

ALPHABETICAL ORDER OF TITLES

The last three digits are merely the general listing of occupations within the first six digits.

EXAMPLE

Occupation: Civil Engineering

D.O.T. Number: 005.061-014

0	Professional, Technical, and Management
00	Engineering
005	Civil Engineering
0	Synthesizing data
6	Speaking-Signaling with people
1	Precision working with things
014	Alphabetical listing of Civil Engineering

Getting to Know Yourself and the World of Work and Education

When we purchase a packaged article, such as a bookcase, from a store and take it home, we expect that it contains a set of instructions on how to assemble the article. As we contemplate our careers and the educational possibilities in which we might become involved, it often seems that there is no packaged program nor are there any specific directions on how to put the various parts together.

Careers impact our lives. Families, geography, self-worth, and lifestyle are all integrated completely with our work. Let's look at families to illustrate this point. Research has shown that families who have traditions in which parents, siblings, aunts, and uncles have careers in semi-skilled work, for example, will generate children who gravitate toward this type of career in their life. The professional family tradition will generate children who are more interested in that area of occupational involvement than others. Another example of how careers influence us is when a change in a parent's career affects where the family will live, with whom they will associate, the financial resources available, and school involvement.

As we look into our personal possibilities for future career connections, we screen everything through two important filters. First is the filter of self-awareness. Second is the filter of our knowledge about the world of education and work. Decision making is the process of integrating what we know of ourselves with what we know about the world, then identifying those careers or technical majors that are both acceptable and accessible to us.

In this section, you will be able to see yourself in light of

1. Your occupational personality style
2. School courses you like and dislike
3. Your interest areas
4. Functions you like related to working with data, people, or things

For each of the four topics, use the following chart to identify the areas that you like. Since each of the topics show how it is related to technical majors and work areas, going through the exercises will show a pattern. Finding those majors and career areas that continually "show up" for you can direct you toward more information in the rest of this book.

Look over the following **Personal Summary Chart**, then proceed through the rest of Part Four. If it is easier, make a copy of the **Personal Summary Chart** to work from.

PERSONAL SUMMARY CHART

Name _____ Date _____

TOPICS	TECHNICAL MAJORS	GOE WORK GROUPS
Write in the answers that most closely describe you.	Below, list the technical majors that relate to your answers in the topic section.	Below, list the GOE work groups that relate to your answers in the topic section.

My Occupational Personality Styles

1 _____   _____   _____
2 _____   _____   _____
3 _____   _____   _____

School Subject Areas That I Like Most

1 _____   _____   _____
2 _____   _____   _____
3 _____   _____   _____

My Highest Interest Work Groups

1 _____   _____   _____
2 _____   _____   _____
3 _____   _____   _____

I am "High," "Medium," or "Low" in being good at and enjoying working with data, people, or things

_____ Data

_____ People

_____ Things

For decades people have been trying to match people to jobs. A particularly helpful development occurred when the idea of personality types emerged. The notion is that specific personality types can be identified in people. There are also careers that harmonize with particular personality types. When a person is successful in becoming aware of what they are like and finding a technical major and subsequent careers that parallel their inclinations, several very positive consequences occur. Some of them are:

1. Self-confidence
2. Self-worth
3. Greater contributions to _____
4. Ability to handle discouragement and obstacles
5. Good relationships with peers and supervisors
6. Feelings of self-fulfillment
7. Fewer illnesses and lower absenteeism
8. General feeling of control over life
9. Less feeling of stress and strain
10. General aura of joy and fascination with life

Seven occupational personality styles can be identified. We all have each of these styles in us; however, we typically peak out in two or three in particular.

Their descriptions are as follows:

Artistic Enjoys expressing oneself; unorganized; unstructured; not particularly sociable except to selected people; enthusiastic about one's activities

Detail-oriented Persistent; enjoys routine and structure; slow to change; intense about beliefs; looks to authority; hardworking

Influencing Sees self as persuasive; good communicator; plans and organizes; entrepreneurial; likes to risk; not particularly academic; action-oriented

Scientific Deals in abstractions and symbols; sometimes appears cynical; curious; analytical; doesn't need a lot of friends; careful in one's work

Serving Persuasively helps others; not necessarily gregarious; altruistic; likes to present and teach; introspective; sensitive to others

Social Enjoys being around people; sees self as an effective communicator; solves problems by asking what others think; interaction is more important than task accomplishment

Technical Solves problems by working with concrete objects; genuine; frank; athletically oriented; not too social with a lot of people; slow to change

When one identifies which two or three styles most closely describe him or her, it is a big step toward locating jobs acceptable to preferred lifestyle and personal inclinations.

OCCUPATIONAL PERSONALITY STYLES AND THEIR RELATIONSHIP TO TECHNICAL MAJORS AND CAREERS

Style	Technical Majors	GOE Work Groups

Artistic

	Cosmetology and Barbering	Barber and Beauty Services
	Fashion Design Technology	09.02
	Graphic Arts	Craft Arts 01.06
	Interior Design	Crafts 05.10
	Jewelry Design and Metal	Performing Arts: Dance
	Smithing	01.05
	Photography	Visual Arts 01.02

Detail-oriented

	Bookkeeping	Administrative Detail 07.01
	Court Reporting	Clerical Machine Operation
	Information Technology	07.06
	and Data Processing	Clerical Handling 07.07
	Law Enforcement	Contracts and Claims 11.12
	Library-Media Technology	Financial Detail 07.03
	Medical Assistant	Finance 11.06
	Medical-Dental Secretary	Mathematical Detail 07.02
	Paralegal Services	Oral Communications 07.04
	Secretarial Science	Records Processing 07.05
		Regulations Enforcement
		11.10

Influencing

	Broadcasting	Business Administration
	Communications	11.05
	Business Management	Business Management 11.11
	Dance Instruction	Communications 11.08
	Farm Management	General Sales 08.02
	Hotel Management	Hospitality Services 09.01
	Journalism	Managerial Work:
	Law Enforcement	Mechanical 05.02

Style	Technical Majors	GOE Work Groups

Influencing

Real Estate

Travel and Tourism

Managerial Work: Plants
and Animals 03.01

Promotion 11.09

Sales Technology 08.01

Scientific

Dietetic Technology

Electronics Technology

Emergency Medical
Technology

Engineering Technology

Environmental Technology

Fire Science

Machine Technology

Mechanical Technology

Medical Technology

Nursing

Surgical Technology

Engineering Technology
05.03

Laboratory Technology 02.04

Life Sciences 02.02

Medical Sciences 02.03

Nursing, Therapy, and
Specialized Teaching
Services 10.02

Physical Sciences 02.01

Serving

Dance Instruction

Food Service

Law Enforcement

Nursing, Licensed
Practical

Hospitality Services 09.01

Nursing, Therapy, and
Specialized Teaching
Services 10.02

Regulations Enforcement
11.10

Safety and Law Enforcement
04.01

Social

Cosmetology and Barbering

Dance Instruction

Barber and Beauty
Services 09.02

Performing Arts: Dance
01.05

Technical

Automotive Body
Repair

Automotive Technology

Aviation Maintenance
Technology

Broadcasting Technology

Cabinetmaking

Carpentry

Computer Maintenance

Crafts 05.10

Craft Technology 05.05

Managerial Work:
Mechanical 05.02

Managerial Work:
Plants and Animals 03.01

Engineering Technology
05.03

Equipment Operation 05.11

Technical

Construction Technology	Laboratory Technology 02.04
Dairy Production Management	Land and Water Vehicle Operation 05.08
Dental Assistance	Medical Sciences 02.03
Dental Technology	Physical Sciences 02.01
Diesel Technology	Production Technology 06.01
Drafting Technology	
Electronics Repair	Quality Control 05.07
Farm Management	
Fire Science	
Food Services	
Heating, Ventilation, and Air Conditioning Technology	
Heavy-Equipment Operations	
Jewelry Design and Metal Smithing	
Machine Technology	
Manufacturing Technology	
Mechanical Technology	
Nurse's Aide	
Plastics Technology	
Plumbing	
Printing Technology	
Radiological Technology	
Surveying	
Telecommunications Technology	
Tool and Die Design	
Truck Driving	
Welding Technology	

COURSES

How well people like their high school courses predict fairly well how they will enjoy similar courses in advanced educational programs. Most people also earn their highest grades in post secondary courses similar to the high school courses in which they did well. We tend to gravitate to those majors that are compatible and will direct us toward desirable career opportunities.

It will help to identify the courses you enjoyed and look at related technical majors and career areas that may be relevant.

SCHOOL SUBJECTS AND THEIR RELATIONSHIP TO TECHNICAL MAJORS AND CAREERS

Course Category	Technical Majors	GOE Work Groups
Business	Bookkeeping	Administrative Detail 07.01
	Business Management	Business Administration
	Dairy Products	11.05
	Management	Business Management
	Farm Management	11.11
	Food Service	Clerical Machine
	Hotel Management	Operation 07.06
	Information Technology	Clerical
	and Data Processing	Handling 07.07
	Medical-Dental Secretary	Contracts and
	Real Estate	Claims 11.12
	Retailing and Marketing	Hospitality Services 09.01
	Secretarial Science	Records Processing
	Transportation	07.05
	Management	Sales Technology
	Travel and Tourism	08.01
Fine Arts	Dance Instruction*	Performing Arts:
	Photography	Dance 01.05
		Visual Arts 01.02
Language Arts	Broadcasting	Communications
	Communications	11.08
	Information Technology	Literary Arts
	and Data Processing	01.01
	Journalism	
Mathematics	Bookkeeping	Engineering 05.01
	Electronics Technology	Engineering
	Engineering Technology	Technology 05.03
	Manufacturing	Mathematical Detail 07.02
	Technology	Mathematics and
	Mechanical Technology	Statistics 11.01
	Retailing and Marketing	

Course Category	Technical Majors	GOE Work Groups

Natural and Physical Sciences

Dental Technology
Environmental Technology
Medical Technology
Nursing, Licensed Practical
Surgical Technology

Laboratory Technology 02.04
Life Sciences 02.02
Managerial Work: Plants and Animals 03.01
Medical Sciences 02.03
Nursing, Therapy, and Specialized Teaching Services 10.02

Physical Education

Dance Instruction

Performing Arts: Dance 01.05

Social Science

Journalism

Communications 11.08
Literary Arts 01.02

Vocational

Automotive Body Repair
Automotive Technology
Aviation Maintenance Technology
Broadcasting Technology
Cabinetmaking
Carpentry
Computer Maintenance
Construction Technology
Cosmetology and Barbering
Court Reporting
Dental Assistance
Dietetic Technology
Drafting Technology
Electrician
Electronics Repair
Fashion Design Technology
Fire Science
Heating, Ventilation, and Air Conditioning Technology
Information Technology and Data Processing
Law Enforcement
Library-Media Technology
Machine Technology
Mechanical Technology

Barber and Beauty Services 09.02
Crafts 05.10
Craft Technology 05.05
Land and Water Vehicle Operation 05.08
Production Technology 06.01
Production Work 06.02
Quality Control 05.07
Security Services 04.02

Course Category	Technical Majors	GOE Work Groups

Vocational

Medical Assistant
Medical-Dental Secretary
Nurse's Aide
Paralegal Services
Printing Technology
Radiological Technology
Secretarial Science
Truck Driving
Welding Technology

YOUR INTEREST AREAS

Different people like different things. Likes are based in part on the experiences you have had and how well you enjoyed them. There may also be areas of interest which you know little about or with which you have had little experience.

As you explore educational majors and various occupations, it is important to look at your interests and compare them with various occupations or categories of occupations. A government task force has identified 12 categories of interests. Each category is further divided into work groups. In total there are 66 work groups. Each work group is described and typical jobs are listed. The various interest areas and work groups are coded and included in the *Complete Guide for Occupational Exploration* (CGOE).

Thirty-five work groups are closely associated with majors found on typical technical college campuses. They are described below.

ARTISTIC 01 *Creatively expressing your ideas or feelings*

Literary Arts 01.01
Working with written expression such as editing, creative writing, critiquing, or publishing
Visual Arts 01.02
Creating original art through studio work, commercial art instructing, and directing
Performing Arts: Dance 01.05
Contributing to dance through performance, instruction, and choreography
Craft Arts 01.06
Applying artistic methods to decorate, create, reproduce, and restore articles dealing with photography, wood, clay, stone, gems, and painting

SCIENTIFIC 02 *Analyzing information gathered through research to solve problems in the natural world*

Life Sciences 02.02
Understanding living things through animal specialization, plant specialization, and food research

Medical Sciences 02.03
Relieving human or animal distress by means of dentistry, veterinary medicine, health specialties, services, and surgery

Laboratory Technology 02.04
Assisting physical scientists or life scientists by conducting and recording research for them

PLANTS AND ANIMALS 03 *Studying plants and animals in their natural environment*

Managerial Work: Plants and Animals 03.01
Managing businesses that deal with plants and animals such as farming, specialty breeding, specialty cropping, forestry, and logging

PROTECTIVE 04 *Guarding the lives and property of others*

Safety and Law Enforcement 04.01
Compelling others to obey the laws through positions in management and investigation

Security Services 04.02
Working to protect people and animals by investigating, enforcing laws, and preventing crimes and fires

MECHANICAL 05 *Using hands and tools to create or repair objects*

Engineering 05.01
Generating and carrying out ideas for construction projects in research, environmental protection, systems design, sales engineering testing, quality control, design, general engineering, work planning and utilization

Managerial Work: Mechanical 05.02
Managing technical jobs in industrial settings

Engineering Technology 05.03
Gathering information for others as a surveyor, drafter, expediter, and coordinator in the areas of petroleum, electrical-electronic industry, mechanics, environmental control, packaging, and storing

Craft Technology 05.05
Working in highly skilled technical areas using tools and nonmanufacturing machinery

28638

Quality Control 05.07
Checking products for compliance with set standards in the mechanical, electrical, environmental, petroleum, structural, logging, and lumber fields

Land and Water Vehicle Operation 05.08
Driving and operating small- to large-sized vehicles, typically for delivering products or services

Crafts 05.10
Working in shops, hotels, and repair shops to create, install, or repair products

INDUSTRIAL 06 *Applying skills to perform repetitive, structured tasks*

Production Technology 06.01
Setting up and operating complex and precise functions with machinery

Production Work 06.02
Feeding, operating, and attending to machines and equipment that do routine, simple work

BUSINESS DETAIL 07 *Carrying out specified tasks in an office setting*

Administrative Detail 07.01
Tending to the clerical work in an office through interviewing, administration, secretarial work, financial work, certifying, investigation, and test administration

Mathematical Detail 07.02
Overseeing the mathematical details in an office through statistical reporting and analysis, accounting, billing, rate computation, payroll, timekeeping, bookkeeping, and book auditing

Oral Communication 07.04
Giving and receiving information in person, or through radio, or by telephone

Records Processing 07.05
Preparing, distributing, and maintaining the accuracy of information documents

Clerical Machine Operations 07.06
Using machines such as computers and keyboard machines to organize data

SELLING 08 *Presenting goods or services to people and persuading them to purchase*

Sales Technology 08.01
Selling technical products and services and consulting with customers about purchasing and sales

ACCOMMODATING 09 *Caring for the needs of others*

Hospitality Services 09.01
Assisting people in their travel and recreational activities
Barber and Beauty Services 09.02
Providing services dealing with hair styling and other cosmetic functions

HUMANITARIAN 10 *Caring for the health needs of others*

Nursing, Therapy, and Specialized Teaching Services 10.02
Aiding in improving the physical and emotional health of others as a nurse, therapist, or teacher

LEADING-INFLUENCING 11 *Using leadership abilities and other skills to guide people in thought and action*

Mathematics and Statistics 11.01
Applying mathematical skills in data processing design and data analysis
Educational and Library Services 11.02
Working in an educational setting as a librarian or as a teacher of subjects such as home economics and vocational studies
Law 11.04
Attending to the legal matters of others through legal practice, document preparation, justice administration, and conciliation
Business Administration 11.05
Making decisions and supervising others in government and nongovernment establishments
Communications 11.08
Working with the media such as editing, writing, broadcasting, translating, and interpreting factual information
Promotion 11.09
Presenting products and services in an appealing manner and raising money through sales, fund membership solicitation, and public relations
Business Management 11.11
Supervising all aspects of a business in such areas as lodging, recreation, amusement, transportation, services, and wholesale–retail

GOE WORK GROUPS AND THEIR RELATIONSHIP TO TECHNICAL MAJORS

Interest Area	GOE Work Groups	Technical Majors
Artistic 01		
	Literary Arts 01.01	Journalism
	Visual Arts 01.02	Fashion Design Technology Graphic Arts Interior Design Photography
	Performing Arts: Dance 01.05	Dance Instruction
	Craft Arts 01.06	Jewelry Design and Metal Smithing
Scientific 02		
	Life Sciences 02.02	Dairy Products Management Dietetic Technology
	Medical Sciences 02.03	Dental Technology Dietetic Technology Medical Technology Nursing, Licensed Practical
	Laboratory Technology 02.04	Dental Technology Medical Technology Radiological Technology
Plants and Animals 03		
	Managerial Work 03.01	Dairy Products Management Farm Management
Protective 04		
	Safety and Law Enforcement 04.01	Fire Science Law Enforcement
	Security Services 04.02	Fire Science Law Enforcement
Mechanical 05		
	Engineering 05.01	Engineering Technology Environmental Technology

Interest Area	GOE Work Groups	Technical Majors

Mechanical 05

	Managerial Work 05.02	Automotive Technology
		Aviation Maintenance
		Technology
		Manufacturing Technology
		Mechanical Technology
		Plastics Technology
		Printing Technology
	Engineering Technology 05.03	Drafting Technology
		Electronics Technology
		Environmental Technology
		Manufacturing Technology
		Mechanical Technology
		Surveying
	Craft Technology 05.05	Automotive Body Repair
		Cabinetmaking
		Carpentry
		Computer Maintenance
		Construction Technology
		Dental Assistance
		Diesel Technology
		Electrician
		Electronics Repair
		Heating, Ventilation, and
		Air Conditioning Technology
		Jewelry Design and
		Metal Smithing
		Medical Assistant
	Quality Control 05.07	Construction Technology
		Diesel Technology
		Electronics Technology
		Engineering Technology
		Machine Technology
		Mechanical Technology
	Land and Water Vehicle Operation 05.08	Heavy-Equipment Operations
		Truck Driving
	Crafts 05.10	Automotive Repair
		Carpentry
		Plumbing
		Welding Technology

The Career Connection for Technical Education

Interest Area	GOE Work Groups	Technical Majors

Industrial 06

Production Technology 06.01 — Machine Technology / Mechanical Technology

Production Work 06.02 — Printing Technology / Welding Technology

Business Detail 07

Administrative Detail 07.01 — Court Reporting / Information Technology and Data Processing / Medical-Dental Secretary / Paralegal Services / Secretarial Science

Mathematical Detail 07.02 — Bookkeeping

Oral Communications 07.04 — Broadcasting Communications / Secretarial Science / Telecommunications Technology

Records Processing 07.05 — Information Technology and Data Processing / Medical-Dental Secretary / Secretarial Science

Selling 08

Sales Technology 08.01 — Real Estate / Retailing and Marketing

Accommodating 09

Hospitality Services 09.01 — Food Services / Hotel Management / Travel and Tourism

Barber and Beauty Services 09.02 — Cosmetology and Barbering

Humanitarian 10

Nursing, Therapy, and Specialized Teaching Services 10.02 — Nursing, Licensed Practical

Leading–Influencing 11

Mathematics and Statistics 11.01 — Retailing and Marketing

Interest Area	GOE Work Groups •	Technical Majors

Leading–Influencing 11

	Educational and Library Services 11.02	Library-Media Technology
	Law 11.04	Court Reporting Paralegal Services
	Business Administration 11.05	Business Management Transportation Management
	Communications 11.08	Broadcasting Communications Journalism
	Promotion 11.09	Fashion Merchandising
	Business Management 11.11	Business Management Hotel Management Travel and Tourism

WORKING WITH DATA, PEOPLE, OR THINGS

We perform different functions when working. These functions have been divided into three categories by the government. They are functions dealing with DATA, PEOPLE, or THINGS.

We all have our individual preferences for the types of functions we enjoy and at which we perceive ourselves as doing well. For example, Jed enjoys working with equipment (THINGS) but doesn't particularly relish the idea of presenting ideas to groups or individuals (PEOPLE). Sherry, on the other hand, likes to teach (PEOPLE) and can work for long periods of times on reports for her students (DATA). Give Steve a computer (DATA) and an assignment to design and build a building (THINGS), and he experiences pure joy.

As you contemplate which careers or training would appeal to you, consider these three major functions and how you see yourself becoming heavily involved with them. It is beneficial to locate those jobs that are not only high in your particular areas of interests and inclinations but also those that are low in the areas of your least desires.

Below, each category is divided into high (abbreviated H in the career outlooks), medium (M), or low (L) levels and is accompanied by the types of activities relevant to each level.

DATA–High	Synthesizing, Coordinating
DATA–Medium	Analyzing, Compiling
DATA–Low	Computing, Copying, Comparing

PEOPLE–High	Mentoring, Negotiating, Instructing
PEOPLE–Medium	Supervising, Diverting, Persuading
PEOPLE–Low	Speaking, Serving, Taking Instructions
THINGS–High	Setting Up, Precision Work
THINGS–Medium	Operating, Driving, Manipulating
THINGS–Low	Tending, Feeding, Handling

When you look at the DOT codes, the middle three numbers represent the DPT levels. The first digit represents DATA; the second, PEOPLE; and the third; THINGS. The higher the number, the more specialized and complex the level of activities required for the particular job.

DATA — PEOPLE — THINGS AND THEIR RELATIONSHIP TO TECHNICAL MAJORS AND CAREERS

Category	Technical Majors	GOE Work Groups
DATA —High	Bookkeeping	Administrative Detail 07.01
	Broadcasting Communications	Clerical Handling 07.07
	Business Management	Communications 11.08
	Court Reporting	Contracts and Claims 11.12
	Drafting Technology	Educational and Library Services 11.02
	Electronics Technology	Engineering 05.01
	Emergency Medical Technology	Engineering Technology 05.03
	Engineering Technology	Laboratory Technology 02.04
	Environmental Technology	Life Sciences 02.02
	Hotel Management	Literary Arts 01.01
	Information Technology and Data Processing	Mathematical Detail 07.02
	Interior Design	Mathematics and Statistics 11.01
	Journalism	Medical Sciences 02.03
	Law Enforcement	Nursing, Therapy, and Specialized Teaching Services 10.02
	Library-Media Technology	
	Manufacturing Technology	
	Mechanical Technology	
	Medical-Dental Secretary	
	Medical Technology	

Category	Technical Majors	GOE Work Groups
DATA —High	Nursing, Licensed Practical Paralegal Services Photography Plastics Technology Radiological Technology Real Estate Retailing and Marketing Secretarial Science Surgical Technology Surveying Telecommunications Technology Transportation Management Travel and Tourism	Oral Communications 07.04 Promotion 11.09 Records Processing 07.05
PEOPLE —High	Broadcasting Communications Cosmetology and Barbering Dance Instruction Farm Management Hotel Management Interior Design	Business Administration 11.05 Business Management 11.11 Educational and Library Services 11.02 General Sales 08.02 Hospitality Services 09.01 Nursing, Therapy, and Specialized Teaching Services 10.02 Oral Communications 07.04 Promotion 11.09 Sales Technology 08.01
THINGS —High	Automotive Repair Automotive Technology Cabinetmaking Carpentry Computer Maintenance Construction Technology Cosmetology and Barbering Court Reporting	Clerical Machine Operation 07.06 Crafts 05.01 Craft Technology 05.05 Engineering Technology 05.03 Land and Water Vehicle Operation 05.08

Category	Technical Majors	GOE Work Groups
THINGS —High	Dairy Products Management	Performing Arts: Dance 01.05
	Dental Assistance	Production Technology 06.01
	Dental Technology	Production Work 06.02
	Diesel Technology	
	Drafting Technology	
	Electrician	
	Electronics Repair	
	Electronics Technology	
	Farm Management	
	Fashion Design Technology	
	Heating, Ventilation, and Air Conditioning Technology	
	Heavy-Equipment Operations	
	Information Technology and Data Processing	
	Interior Design	
	Jewelry Design and Metal Smithing	
	Machine Technology	
	Manufacturing Technology	
	Mechanical Technology	
	Medical Technology	
	Photography	
	Plastics Technology	
	Plumbing	
	Printing Technology	
	Radiological Technology	
	Secretarial Science	
	Telecommunications Technology	
	Tool and Die Design	
	Truck Driving	
	Welding Technology	

Technical Majors and Their Career Opportunities

Automotive Body Repair

Auto body technicians restore damaged automobiles to original conditions. They straighten bent structures, remove dents, and replace damaged parts. They use special equipment to straighten frames and body structures. Auto body technicians work with fiberglass, plastic, and sheet metal. Technicians refinish repairs to match the original color of the automobile. Auto body technicians may also work as claims adjusters for insurance companies. Technicians normally are employed in auto body repair shops and fleet garages.

EDUCATIONAL REQUIREMENTS

Auto body technicians have three educational options available. They may complete a two-year program leading to an Associate of Science degree or an Associate of Applied Science degree. Some educational institutions offer one-year programs leading to a certificate of completion. They may also be hired by auto body repair shops as apprentices where they may learn the trade through on-the-job training.

COURSE REQUIREMENTS

Auto Body and Frame Alignment
Automotive Body Repair
Automotive Finishing Preparation
    and Painting
Automotive Glass Replacement
Automotive Plastics
Automotive Repair (basic
    and advanced)
Automotive Wiring Systems

Body Panel Replacement
Estimating
Fiberglass Repair
Heat Treatment
Technical Mathematics
Welding and Cutting
Wheel and Axle Alignment

RECOMMENDED HIGH SCHOOL COURSES

Automotive Shop
English

Mathematics
Metal Shop

CAREERS	D.O.T. NUMBERS	OUTLOOK	AVERAGE INITIAL SALARIES
Aircraft Body Repairer	807.261-010	Excellent	$21,800
Auto Body Customizer	807.361-010	Excellent	26,700
Auto Body Repair Supervisor	807.137-010	Good	28,000
Auto Body Repairer	807.381-010	Excellent	18,100
Railroad Car Repairer	622.381-014	Fair	17,800

Occupational Personality Styles: Technical, Detail-oriented

DPT Functions: Data = M   People = L   Things = H

GOE Work Groups: Crafts, Craft Technology

Automotive Technology

Auto mechanics use diagnostic equipment to determine malfunctions and mechanical problems in automobiles. They adjust, repair, or replace parts as needed. Generalists are interested in overall auto operations. Specialists concentrate on specific tasks such as tune-ups or repairing brakes, transmissions, or engines. Auto mechanics may work in auto repair shops, auto dealerships, or fleet garages.

EDUCATIONAL REQUIREMENTS

Auto mechanics may complete a two-year program leading to an Associate of Science degree or an Associate of Applied Science degree. Many mechanics complete a one-year trade school program leading to a certificate of completion. Many mechanics are self-taught or learn the profession through on-the-job training. Some states require mechanics to be licensed.

COURSE REQUIREMENTS

Auto Shop Management
Auto Shop Safety
Automotive Air-Conditioning
  Systems
Automotive Electrical Systems
Automotive Engine Rebuilding
Automotive Engine Theory
Blueprint Reading
Brakes and Alignment

Drive Train Components
Fuel Systems
Lubrication
Suspension and Steering
Technical Mathematics
Transmissions
Tune-up and Emission Control
Welding

RECOMMENDED HIGH SCHOOL COURSES

Auto Shop
Drafting
English

Industrial Arts
Mathematics

CAREERS	D.O.T. NUMBERS	OUTLOOK	AVERAGE INITIAL SALARIES
Auto Mechanic	620.261-010	Excellent	$18,200
Auto Mechanic Apprentice	620.261-012	Good	19,100
Engine Repairer	625.281-018	Good	15,000
Engine Repair Supervisor	625.131-014	Good	21,300
Exhaust Emissions Technician	599.382-014	Excellent	15,000
Experimental Mechanic	621.261-022	Good	25,300
Farm Equipment Mechanic	624.281-010	Good/Exc.	16,900
Farm Machinery Set-up Mechanic	624.381-018	Fair	16,300
Fuel Injection Mechanic	625.281-022	Excellent	18,200
Garage Supervisor	620.131-014	Good	24,000
Industrial Mechanic	620.281-050	Excellent	19,600
Motorcycle Repair Supervisor	620.131-018	Fair	17,900
Small Engine Mechanic	625.281-034	Good	15,100
Tractor Mechanic	620.281-058	Good	18,200
Tune-up Mechanic	620.281-066	Excellent	18,200

Occupational Personality Styles: Technical, Scientific

DPT Functions: Data = H   People = M   Things = H

GOE Work Groups: Crafts, Craft Technology

Aviation Maintenance Technology

Aviation maintenance technicians maintain, inspect, and repair aircraft components. They dismantle engines, check for damage, and replace worn parts. They inspect aircraft structures for signs of damage and stress. Technicians overhaul and inspect the entire aircraft and repair damage to all airframe components and systems. Technicians may also be known as power-plant mechanics and airplane mechanics. Employment opportunities exist with airlines, aerospace manufacturers, military forces, and airport maintenance departments. Aviation maintenance technicians may also work as technical writers, field representatives, aircraft inspectors, quality control inspectors, and airframe/power-plant instructors.

EDUCATIONAL REQUIREMENTS

Aviation maintenance technicians normally complete a two-year program at aviation schools leading to an Associate of Science degree or an Associate of Applied Science degree. Technicians must also pass the Federal Aviation Administration (FAA) oral and written exam for an airframe and power-plant (A&P) license.

COURSE REQUIREMENTS

AC and DC Electricity
Aircraft Drawing
Airframe Inspection
Airframe Mechanics
Cabin Atmosphere Control
  Systems
Communication and Navigation
  Systems
Corrosion Control
Electrical Systems
Engine Overhaul and Inspection
Fire Protection Systems
Fuel Systems

Hydraulics
Ignition Systems
Instrument Systems
Landing Systems
Mathematics
Physics
Pneumatics
Power-Plant Mechanics
Propellers
Reciprocation Engines
Sheet Metal
Weight and Balance
Welding

RECOMMENDED HIGH SCHOOL COURSES

Auto Shop
Drafting
Electrical Shop
English

Industrial Arts
Mathematics
Metal Shop
Physics

CAREERS	D.O.T. NUMBERS	OUTLOOK	AVERAGE INITIAL SALARIES
Aircraft Maintenance Supervisor	621.131-014	Excellent	28,000
Airframe and Power-Plant Mechanic	621.281-014	Excellent	$26,800
Experimental Mechanic	621.261-022	Excellent	27,500
Field Service Mechanic	621.281-014	Excellent	26,800
Flight Test Mechanic	621.281-014	Excellent	27,800
Rocket Engine Mechanic	621.281-030	Excellent	28,200
Supercharger Repair Supervisor	621.131-010	Excellent	33,000

Occupational Personality Styles: Technical, Scientific

DPT Functions: Data = H   People = M   Things = H

GOE Work Groups: Crafts, Craft Technology

Bookkeeping

Bookkeepers record and classify business data. They post transactions to journals and ledgers. They may also do payroll, accounts payable, accounts receivable, and cost accounting record keeping. They may work as office managers or accounting technicians as well. Employment opportunities may be found in virtually all businesses, organizations, and government offices.

EDUCATIONAL REQUIREMENTS

Bookkeepers and accounting technicians may complete a two-year program leading to an Associate of Science degree or an Associate of Business degree. Many bookkeepers and entry-level accounting clerks complete a trade-school program of up to one year, leading to a certificate of completion.

COURSE REQUIREMENTS

Accounting
Budgeting
Business Communications
Business Law
Business Management
Business Mathematics
College Algebra
Cost Accounting

Data Processing
Database Management
Economics
English
Information Systems
Introduction to Computers
Psychology
Tax Accounting

RECOMMENDED HIGH SCHOOL COURSES

Accounting
Bookkeeping
Business Law
Business Machine Operations
Business Mathematics

Computer Operations
Data Processing
English
Mathematics
Typing/Word Processing

CAREERS	D.O.T. NUMBERS	OUTLOOK	AVERAGE INITIAL SALARIES
Audit Clerk	210.382-010	Excellent	$16,000
Audit Clerk Supervisor	210.132-010	Good	19,300
Bookkeeper I	210.382-014	Excellent	20,300
Bookkeeper II	210.382-014	Excellent	17,500
Reconciliation Clerk	210.382-010	Excellent	16,000

Occupational Personality Style: Detail-oriented

DPT Functions: Data = H   People = L   Things = L

GOE Work Groups: Clerical Machine Operation, Clerical Handling, Mathematical Detail

Broadcasting Communications

Broadcasters are the voice of radio and television stations. They deliver news and live commercials, introduce programs, and play recorded music. Some broadcasters may act as talk show hosts, weather announcers, or sportscasters. Broadcasters operate radio and television control boards and audio-switching equipment. Some broadcasters may be employed as advertising salespeople. Employment opportunities are found with radio and television stations.

EDUCATIONAL REQUIREMENTS

Broadcasters may complete a two-year program leading to an Associate of Science degree. Broadcasting schools offer training which may vary from several weeks to several months. Before being employed, a broadcaster must successfully pass the FCC licensing examination.

COURSE REQUIREMENTS

Applied Broadcasting	Media Sales
Audio Production Techniques	Music Production
Basic AC and DC Electronics	News Reporting
Broadcast Delivery	Public Speaking
Copywriting	Radio and TV Production
English	Radio and TV Sales
Introduction to Broadcasting	Radio and TV Speaking

RECOMMENDED HIGH SCHOOL COURSES

English (3 years or more)	Journalism
Fine Arts	Speech

CAREERS	D.O.T. NUMBERS	OUTLOOK	AVERAGE INITIAL SALARIES
Announcer	159.147-010	Good	$30,100
Announcer, International	159.147-010	Fair	Varies
Assignment Editor	132.132-010	Good	19,900
Commentator	131.067-010	Good	19,800
Disc Jockey	159.147-014	Fair	Varies
Local Announcer	159.347-010	Good	19,900
Narrator	150.147-010	Fair	18,700
Network Announcer	159.147-010	Excellent	18,600
News Analyst	131.067-010	Excellent	21,600
Newscaster	131.262-010	Good	19,900
News Director	184.167-014	Good	28,600
Newswriter	131.262-014	Good	18,000
Reporter	131.262-018	Excellent	18,800
Sports Announcer	159.347-010	Excellent	Varies

Occupational Personality Styles: Social, Technical, Influencing

DPT Functions: Data = H   People = H   Things = L

GOE Work Groups: Crafts, Communications

Broadcasting Technology

Broadcast technicians operate and maintain radio and television transmission equipment. They also operate and maintain equipment used to regulate sound and picture quality. They operate audio mixers, video-switches and cameras, microphones, and other audio and video equipment. They may also be required to work as on-the-air announcers. Broadcast technicians are sometimes called broadcast engineers. They are employed by VHF and UHF television stations and by AM and FM radio stations.

EDUCATIONAL REQUIREMENTS

Broadcast technicians normally complete a two-year program leading to an Associate of Science degree or an Associate of Applied Science degree. Prior to being employed, broadcast technicians must successfully pass the FCC Class I Radio/Telephone Licensing examination. They may also take the Certified Electronics Technician (CET) examination.

COURSE REQUIREMENTS

AC and DC Electrical Theory
AC and DC Electronic Theory
AM and FM Theory
Antennas and Wave Amplifiers
Audio and RF Amplifiers
Audio and Video Signal
   Modulation
Broadcast Transmitters
Electromagnetics
Electronic Communications

Film Equipment
Microwave Communication Systems
Mathematics
Physics
Power Distribution
Transmission Lines and Wave Guides
TV Systems
Video Monitors
Video Production

RECOMMENDED HIGH SCHOOL COURSES

Electrical Shop
English

Mathematics (3 years or more)
Physics

CAREERS	D.O.T. NUMBERS	OUTLOOK	AVERAGE INITIAL SALARIES
Audio Operator	194.262-010	Good	$20,400
Audio Technician	194.262-010	Excellent	21,100
Camera Operator	143.062-022	Good	20,000
Camera Operator, Special Effects	143.062-022	Good	20,800
Communications Technician	926.362-010	Good	19,100
Dubbing Machine Operator	962.665-010	Excellent	20,200
Engineer, Studio Operations	194.262-018	Good	23,300
Microwave Engineer	193.262-018	Fair/Good	21,500
Sound Effects Manager	962.167-010	Good	24,800
Sound Effects Technician	962.281-014	Good	19,500
Sound Mixer	194.262-018	Excellent	21,300
Sound Recording Technician	194.362-010	Excellent	19,000
Sound Technician	829.281-022	Good	19,000
Transmission Engineer	003.167-030	Good	23,300
Video Engineer	194.282-010	Good	23,300
Videotape Recording Engineer	194.362-010	Excellent	23,000

Occupational Personality Styles: Influencing, Social

DPT Functions: Data = H   People = H   Things = H

GOE Work Groups: Communications, Elemental Arts, Performing Arts: Drama

Business Management

Business managers normally work in small companies or stores. They manage people and resources, supervise workers, and develop work schedules. They may also be involved with professional selling. Business management professionals may work as foremen, supervisors, management trainees, or salespeople. Employment opportunities may be found in real estate, insurance, advertising, marketing, and public relations.

EDUCATIONAL REQUIREMENTS

Business management professionals normally complete a two-year program leading to an Associate of Science degree.

COURSE REQUIREMENTS

Accounting
Advertising
Algebra
Business Communications
Business Law
Business Mathematics
Communications
Communications (organizational behavior)
Cost Accounting

Data Processing
Economics
English
Information Management
Management Decision Making
Management Principles
Marketing
Psychology
Sales
Statistics

RECOMMENDED HIGH SCHOOL COURSES

Accounting
Bookkeeping
Business
Business Law
Business Machine Operations
Computer Operations

Economics
English
Mathematics
Psychology
Typing/Word Processing

CAREERS	D.O.T. NUMBERS	OUTLOOK	AVERAGE INITIAL SALARIES
Administrative Assistant	169.167-010	Good	$18,100
Business Manager	191.117-018	Excellent	21,200
Buyer	162.157-018	Excellent	23,000
Department Manager	187.167-042	Excellent	21,200
Export Manager	163.117-014	Excellent	21,200
Fast-Foods Manager	185.137-010	Excellent	23,100
Food Service Manager	187.167-106	Excellent	19,800
Funeral Services Director	187.167-030	Excellent	24,300
Market Manager	186.167-042	Excellent	21,000
Merchandise Manager	185.167-034	Excellent	21,000
Purchasing Agent	162.157-038	Good	25,100
Retail Store Manager	185.167-046	Excellent	23,000
Sales Manager	163.167-018	Excellent	24,100
Service Department Manager	187.167-142	Excellent	19,800

Occupational Personality Styles: Influencing, Social

DPT Functions: Data = H   People = H   Things = L

GOE Work Groups: Business Administration, Business Management, General Sales, Hospitality Services

Cabinetmaking

Cabinetmakers cut, shape, and assemble parts to form furniture, office equipment, and cabinets. They also repair damaged furniture. Cabinetmakers read blueprints, estimate construction costs, select materials, and use a variety of woodworking equipment to create cabinets and furniture. Cabinetmakers may work as millwrights or cabinet installers. They may find employment opportunities in furniture factories, with building contractors, or with a self-employed contractor.

EDUCATIONAL REQUIREMENTS

Cabinetmakers may complete a two-year program leading to an Associate of Science degree. More likely, they will be employed as apprentices. Some apprentices may be hired by experienced cabinetmakers and learn the trade through on-the-job training.

COURSE REQUIREMENTS

Blueprint Reading
Cabinet Design
Cabinet Installation
Cabinetmaking Theory
Carpentry
Drafting
Estimation
Hand and Power Tool
    Application

Layout Procedures
Millworking
Small Business Management
Stair Building
Technical Mathematics
    (including Trigonometry)
Woodworking
Woodworking Materials

RECOMMENDED HIGH SCHOOL COURSES

Drafting
English

Mathematics
Wood Shop

The Career Connection for Technical Education

CAREERS	D.O.T. NUMBERS	OUTLOOK	AVERAGE INITIAL SALARIES
Cabinetmaker	660.280-010	Good	$15,500
Cabinetmaker Supervisor	660.130-010	Good	27,500
Furniture Finisher	763.381-010	Fair/Poor	16,300
Machinery Supervisor	669.130-022	Fair	23,000
Machinist, Wood	669.380-014	Good	20,800
Patternmaker, Wood	661.281-022	Fair	19,000

Occupational Personality Styles: Technical, Detail-oriented

DPT Functions: Data = H   People = M   Things = H

GOE Work Groups: Craft Technology, Production Work

Carpentry

Carpenters build and repair buildings. They build forms, walls, roofs, and trims. Rough-work carpenters build frames, joints, and rafters. Finish-work carpenters work on appearance products such as paneling and floors. They read blueprints, estimate costs, select materials, and construct the building. Some carpenters are employed as job foremen and coordinate the activities of subcontractors and other craftsmen. In addition, some carpenters specialize in repair and remodeling of structures. Employment opportunities may be found with building contractors and home builders.

EDUCATIONAL REQUIREMENTS

Carpenters may complete a two-year program leading to an Associate of Science degree. However, in most states, carpenters must complete apprenticeships of up to four years. The apprenticeships are normally controlled by labor unions or labor guilds.

COURSE REQUIREMENTS

Blueprint Reading
Building Estimating
Concrete Fundamentals
Construction Materials
Construction Practices
Construction Project
   Management
Drafting
Exterior and Interior Finishing
Framing
Hand and Power Tool Applications
Home Maintenance and Repair
House Construction
House Wiring
Industrial Plastics
Joinery and Millwork
Materials Science
Mathematics
Residential Estimation
Welding

RECOMMENDED HIGH SCHOOL COURSES

Drafting
Electrical Shop
English
Industrial Arts
Mathematics

Metal Shop
Physics
Trigonometry
Wood Shop

CAREERS	D.O.T. NUMBERS	OUTLOOK	AVERAGE INITIAL SALARIES
Accoustical Carpenter	860.381-010	Fair	$14,500
Apprentice Carpenter	860.381-026	Fair	13,400
Carpenter Supervisor	860.131-018	Excellent	30,000
Construction Carpenter	860.381-022	Excellent	25,400
House Carpenter	860.381-022	Good	25,400
Maintenance Carpenter	860.281-010	Good	22,400
Rough Carpenter	860.381-042	Excellent	20,300
Shipwright Apprentice	860.381-062	Fair	19,500

Occupational Personality Styles: Technical, Detail-oriented

DPT Functions: Data = M   People = L   Things = H

GOE Work Groups: Craft Technology, Production Work

Computer Maintenance

Computer maintenance technicians install and maintain computer systems. They diagnose, repair, and calculate information-gathering systems. They apply troubleshooting procedures to determine malfunctions in computer equipment. They may program computers as part of their job. Computer maintenance technicians may be employed as service technicians, bench or field technicians, or technical representatives. They are usually employed by computer manufacturing or maintenance service firms.

EDUCATIONAL REQUIREMENTS

Computer maintenance technicians normally complete a two-year program leading to an Associate of Science degree or an Associate of Applied Science degree in computer science. They may also take the Certified Electronics Technician (CET) examination.

COURSE REQUIREMENTS

AC and DC Electricity
AC and DC Electronics
Assembly Programming
Circuit Analysis
Computer Architecture
Computer Inputs and Outputs
Computer Memory Systems
Computer Programming
Control Circuits
Data Acquisition Systems

Data Processing Principles
Digital Arithmetic and Logic
Digital Electronic Fundamentals
Digital Interfacing
Electronic Repair
Electronic Test Procedures
Microprocessor Theory
Physics
Timing

RECOMMENDED HIGH SCHOOL COURSES

Computer Operations
Data Processing
Electrical Shop

English
Mathematics

CAREERS	D.O.T. NUMBERS	OUTLOOK	AVERAGE INITIAL SALARIES
Computer Inspector	726.381-010	Excellent	$23,900
Computer Operator	213.362-010	Excellent	18,300
Computer Peripheral Operator	213.382-010	Excellent	18,300
Computer Repairer	829.261-018	Excellent	22,900
Computer Sales and Service Technician	275.257-010	Excellent	18,900

Occupational Personality Styles: Technical, Detail-oriented

DPT Functions: Data = H   People = L   Things = H

GOE Work Group: Craft Technology

Construction Technology

Construction technicians work on commercial, industrial, and residential building sites and on civil engineering projects. They help plan and control building details and coordinate the work of subcontractors and craftsmen. They also help in the actual construction of structures and engineering projects. Technicians perform surveys, cost accounting, and site troubleshooting. They inspect job sites to ensure that materials and dimensions are correct. They may supervise construction crews. Construction technicians normally work for building contractors and construction companies, but they may also work as insurance adjusters for insurance companies and as building inspectors for municipal governments.

EDUCATIONAL REQUIREMENTS

Construction technicians normally complete a two-year program leading to an Associate of Science degree or an Associate of Applied Science degree.

COURSE REQUIREMENTS

Blueprint Reading
Building Codes
Cabinetmaking
Carpentry
Construction Drafting
Construction Estimating
Construction Plastics
Construction Project Management
Drywall Finishing
Energy Conservation
Materials Science
Solar Design

Solar Energy
Specifications and Contracts
Strength of Materials
Structural Engineering
Structural Steel Detailing
Surveying
Technical Mathematics
   (including Trigonometry)
Welding
Wiring Installation
Woodworking

RECOMMENDED HIGH SCHOOL COURSES

Drafting
Electrical Shop
English
Industrial Arts

Mathematics (including
 Trigonometry)
Physics
Wood Shop

CAREERS	D.O.T. NUMBERS	OUTLOOK	AVERAGE INITIAL SALARIES
Assistant Construction Superintendent	869.367-010	Fair	$31,500
Building Construction Inspector	182.267-010	Fair	24,900
Carpenter Supervisor	860.131-018	Excellent	30,000
Contractor	182.167-010	Excellent	Varies
Fabrication Supervisor	769.130-010	Good	23,900
Pipeline Inspector	182.262-010	Fair	20,000
Reinforced Concrete Inspector	182.267-010	Fair	21,000
Road Construction Inspector	859.281-010	Good	26,000
Structural Steel Inspector	182.267-010	Fair	22,000

Occupational Personality Styles: Technical, Influencing

DPT Functions: Data = H People = L Things = H

GOE Work Groups: Crafts, Craft Technology, Production Work

Cosmetology and Barbering

Cosmetologists shampoo, cut, and style hair. They provide cosmetic care for the face, hands, arms, skin, and hair. Cosmetologists also provide makeup analysis for clients and act as beauty consultants. Cosmetologists may be employed in department stores, hospitals, hotels, or hair salons.

Barbers cut, style, and color hair. They may shampoo hair. Barbers also trim mustaches and beards and provide scalp and facial massages. They may also style and care for hair pieces.

EDUCATIONAL REQUIREMENTS

Cosmetologists may complete a two-year program leading to an Associate of Science degree. They may also attend beauty school for up to 2,000 hours. Cosmetologists must successfully pass a state licensing examination before becoming employed.

Barbers may attend a two-year program leading to an Associate of Applied Science degree. They may also attend barber school for approximately 2,000 hours. Barbers must successfully pass a state licensing examination containing written and practice portions before becoming employed as a barber.

COURSE REQUIREMENTS

Anatomy	Makeup
Bacteriology	Manicuring
Basic Hair Care	Personal Grooming
Cosmetology	Salesmanship
First Aid	Salon Management
Hair Cutting	Shampooing
Hair Styling	Skin Care
Hair Tinting	Thermal Chemical Hair Treatment

RECOMMENDED HIGH SCHOOL COURSES

Biology	English
Bookkeeping	Health
Chemistry	Mathematics

CAREERS	D.O.T. NUMBERS	OUTLOOK	AVERAGE INITIAL SALARIES
Barber	330.371-010	Excellent	$14,100
Cosmetologist	332.271-010	Excellent	14,400
Hair Stylist	332.271-018	Good/Fair	12,000

Occupational Personality Styles:	Artistic, Social
DPT Functions:	Data = L People = H Things = H
GOE Work Group:	Barber and Beauty Services

Court Reporting

Court reporters maintain verbatim records of legal proceedings. Using short-hand typing machines, they may work as courtroom reporters or in law firms. They may also do freelance reporting of wills and other records.

EDUCATIONAL REQUIREMENTS

Court reporters generally complete a trade-school program of up to one year. Some court reporters complete a two-year program leading to an Associate of Science degree. Court reporters are generally expected to pass the Registered Professional Reporters (RPR) examination.

COURSE REQUIREMENTS

Anatomy	Introduction to Court Reporting
Business Law	Legal and Medical Terminology
Civil and Criminal Law	Transcription Techniques
English	Typing

RECOMMENDED HIGH SCHOOL COURSES

Business Law	Mathematics
English	Shorthand
Journalism	Typing/Word Processing

CAREER	D.O.T. NUMBER	OUTLOOK	AVERAGE INITIAL SALARY
Court Reporter	202.362-010	Good	$28,100

Occupational Personality Style:	Detail-oriented
DPT Functions:	Data = H People = M Things = M
GOE Work Groups:	Administrative Detail, Clerical Machine Operation

Dairy Products Management

Dairy technicians work in the area of dairy husbandry. They breed and raise dairy cattle, maintain an environment that is healthful for the herds, and supervise the daily milking of the cows. They may market their own dairy products or sell them to dairy cooperatives. Dairy technicians may manage their own herds or work as dairy managers for other farms. Dairy technicians may also work for dairy processors, feed companies, veterinary clinics, or government agencies.

EDUCATIONAL REQUIREMENTS

Dairy technicians normally complete a two-year program leading to an Associate of Science degree. An internship on working dairy farms may be required at some schools.

COURSE REQUIREMENTS

Agricultural Economics
Agricultural Management
Agriculture Mechanics
Calf Management
Chemistry
Crop Production
Dairy Cattle Anatomy

Dairy Cattle Nutrition
Dairy Production Management
Dairy Reproduction
Lactation
Mathematics
Practical Veterinary Skills

RECOMMENDED HIGH SCHOOL COURSES

Agriculture
Biology
Bookkeeping
Botany

Business
Chemistry
English
Mathematics

CAREERS	D.O.T. NUMBERS	OUTLOOK	AVERAGE INITIAL SALARIES
Dairy Farm Manager	040.061-018	Fair	$23,500
Dairy Technologist	040.061-022	Fair	19,100

Occupational Personality Styles: Technical, Detail-oriented

DPT Functions: Data = H   People = M   Things = M

GOE Work Groups: Life Sciences, Managerial Work: Plants and Animals, Quality Control

Dance Instruction

Dance instructors teach dancing in private studios and community recreation centers. They may specialize in specific dance routines, such as ballroom, jazz, or Latin. Some dance instructors teach dance as therapeutic exercise for senior citizens.

EDUCATIONAL REQUIREMENTS

Dance instructors may complete a two-year program leading to an Associate of Science degree. Some instructors may complete dance programs at private studios or commercial dance schools.

COURSE REQUIREMENTS

Aerobic Dancing
Anatomy
Ballet
Ballroom Dance
Dance Teaching Techniques
Folk Dance

Interpersonal Communication
Modern Dance
Physiology
Public Speaking
Social Dance
Square Dance

RECOMMENDED HIGH SCHOOL COURSES

English
Fine Arts

Sociology
Speech

CAREERS	D.O.T. NUMBERS	OUTLOOK	AVERAGE INITIAL SALARIES
Choreographer	151.027-010	Poor	$25,700
Dance Instructor	151.027-014	Fair	16,800
Dance Studio Manager	187.167-086	Fair	18,000
Dancer	151.047-010	Fair	13,500

Occupational Personality Styles: Social, Serving

DPT Functions: Data = M People = H Things = M

GOE Work Groups: Educational and Library Services, Performing Arts: Dance

Dental Assistance

Dental assistants assist dentists in the treatment of patients. They greet patients and make them comfortable, X-ray the patients' mouths and develop the films, assist the dentist, and prepare fillings. Dental assistants also make patient appointments, maintain patient records, and order and maintain dental supplies. Dental assistants may find employment in dental offices, health clinics, hospitals, government agencies, and with dental products manufacturers.

EDUCATIONAL REQUIREMENTS

Dental assistants normally complete a two-year program leading to an Associate of Science degree. They may also attend a dental school for several months to receive a certificate of completion. Dental assistants may also take the Certified Dental Assistant (CDA) examination.

COURSE REQUIREMENTS

Anesthesia
Cardiopulmonary Resuscitation
Clinical Practice
Dental Anatomy
Dental Lab Procedures
Dental Materials
Dental Office Procedure
Dental Radiology
Dental Science
First Aid
Health
Insurance
Microbiology
Nutrition
Office Management
Oral Surgery
Pharmacology
Preventive Dentistry
Psychology

RECOMMENDED HIGH SCHOOL COURSES

Biology
Bookkeeping
Chemistry
English
Health
Mathematics
Psychology

CAREERS	D.O.T. NUMBERS	OUTLOOK	AVERAGE INITIAL SALARIES
Dental Assistant	079.371-018	Excellent	$16,600
Dental Hygienist	078.361-010	Excellent	26,100
Dental Hygienist, Community Health	078.361-010	Good	24,100
Dental Hygienist, Public School	078.361-010	Fair	24,100

Occupational Personality Styles:	Technical, Detail-oriented, Serving
DPT Functions:	Data = H People = M Things = H
GOE Work Groups:	Craft Technology, Medical Sciences

Dental Technology

Dental technicians make dentures, fabricate crowns and inlays, and construct bridges. They also make orthodontic braces. They create delicate dental pieces with their hands, using small instruments. Dental technicians are normally employed in dental laboratories.

EDUCATIONAL REQUIREMENTS

Dental technicians normally attend a trade school for up to one year and receive a certificate of completion.

COURSE REQUIREMENTS

Dental Anatomy   Dental Materials
Dental Lab Procedures   Dental Science

RECOMMENDED HIGH SCHOOL COURSES

Biology   English
Chemistry   Health
Crafts   Physics

CAREERS	D.O.T. NUMBERS	OUTLOOK	AVERAGE INITIAL SALARIES
Dental Ceramist	712.381-042	Good	$17,300
Dental Laboratory Technician	712.381-018	Good	13,600
Dental Technician, Crown and Bridge	712.381-018	Good	23,100
Dental Waxer	712.381-046	Fair	16,000
Denture Model Maker	712.684-046	Good	18,000

Occupational Personality Styles: Technical, Detail-oriented, Serving

DPT Functions: Data = H   People = M   Things = H

GOE Work Groups: Craft Technology, Medical Sciences

Diesel Technology

Diesel mechanics test, adjust, and repair diesel engines. They conduct diagnostic tests and repair and replace parts as needed. Mechanics maintain and repair transmissions, brakes, and lifting units. They may work as bus or heavy-equipment mechanics. Employment opportunities may be found with trucking companies, bus lines, construction companies, farming operations, and power plants.

EDUCATIONAL REQUIREMENTS

Diesel mechanics may complete a two-year program leading to an Associate of Science or Associate of Applied Science degree. In some states, mechanics may complete a four-year apprenticeship instead of attending a technical school. Many mechanics learn the profession through on-the-job training.

COURSE REQUIREMENTS

Diesel Electrical Systems
Diesel Engine Mechanics
Fuel Systems
Hydraulics
Machine Shop
Pneumatic and Hydraulic
   Brake Systems
Power Generation
Power Train Repair and Theory

Steering Systems
Trailer Axle Systems and Under-
   carriages
Truck and Heavy Equipment
   Theory of Operation
Truck and Heavy Equipment
   Transmissions
Welding

RECOMMENDED HIGH SCHOOL COURSES

Auto Shop
English

Industrial Arts
Mathematics

CAREERS	D.O.T. NUMBERS	OUTLOOK	AVERAGE INITIAL SALARIES
Diesel Engine Assembler	806.481-014	Good	$21,500
Diesel Engine Inspector	806.261-010	Fair	26,500
Diesel Engine Mechanic	625.281-010	Excellent	24,700
Diesel Engine Tester	625.261-010	Fair	26,500
Diesel Power-Plant Mechanic	631.261-014	Excellent	24,700
Diesel Power-Plant Supervisor	631.131-010	Good	30,000

Occupational Personality Styles: Technical, Detail-oriented

DPT Functions: Data = H   People = M   Things = H

GOE Work Groups: Craft Technology, Production Work

Dietetic Technology

Dietetic technicians assist dieticians in planning meals. They are generally responsible for food purchases, and they may supervise the preparation and serving of food. They implement dietary plans developed by dieticians and explain the plans to people. Dietetic technicians may find employment in hospitals, schools, health-care centers, and government agencies.

EDUCATIONAL REQUIREMENTS

Dietetic technicians may complete a two-year program leading to an Associate of Science degree. They may also attend a trade school for six to 12 months and receive a certificate of completion.

COURSE REQUIREMENTS

Anatomy
Chemistry
Dietetics
Food Selection and Preparation

Menu Planning
Microbiology
Nutrition

RECOMMENDED HIGH SCHOOL COURSES

Biology
Chemistry
English
Health

Home Economics
Mathematics
Psychology

CAREERS	D.O.T. NUMBERS	OUTLOOK	AVERAGE INITIAL SALARIES
Dietetic Intern	077.124-010	Fair/Poor	$12,500
Dietetic Technician	077.124-010	Fair	17,000
Food Products Tester	029.361-014	Fair	17,000

Occupational Personality Styles: Scientific, Detail-oriented, Serving

DPT Functions: Data = H   People = H   Things = L

GOE Work Groups: Life Sciences, Medical Sciences

Drafting Technology

Drafting technicians produce drawings that show dimensions and specifications based on rough sketches, specifications, and calculations submitted by engineers, designers, or architects. They may use either computer-aided design (CAD) systems or traditional drafting equipment. They calculate the strength, quality, and costs of materials to be used. Technicians must be able to do neat, legible lettering, tracing work, and engineering changes. They must also have skills in technical illustration. Drafting technicians normally specialize in electrical, architectural, civil, or mechanical drafting. Employment possibilities are found in private industry, municipal governments, construction companies, and architectural firms.

EDUCATIONAL REQUIREMENTS

Drafting technicians normally complete a two-year program leading to an Associate of Science degree or an Associate of Applied Science degree.

COURSE REQUIREMENTS

AC and DC Electrical Theory
Architectural Drafting
Architectural Drawing
Architectural Graphics
Automation and Computerized
   Numerical Control
Building Codes
Civil Drafting
Civil Engineering
Computer-Aided Design
Construction Estimating
Drafting
Electrical Drafting

Electromechanical Drafting
Hydraulics and Pneumatics
Machine Drafting
Machine Tool Operation
Materials Science
Mathematics (including
   Trigonometry)
Mechanical Drafting
Physics
Production Processes
Strength of Materials
Structural Engineering
Tool and Die Drafting

RECOMMENDED HIGH SCHOOL COURSES

Computer Operation
Drafting
English

Mathematics (including
Trigonometry)
Physics

CAREERS	D.O.T. NUMBERS	OUTLOOK	AVERAGE INITIAL SALARIES
Architectural Drafter	001.261-010	Good	$18,100
Automotive Design Layout	017.281-026	Good	18,500
Detail Drafter	017.261-030	Good	16,900
Drafter Apprentice	017.281-014	Good	14,000
Electrical Drafter	003.281-010	Good	17,600
Geological Drafter	010.281-014	Fair/Good	17,900
Heating and Ventilation Drafter	017.261-034	Fair	18,500
Landscape Drafter	001.261-014	Good	17,200
Plumbing Drafter	017.261-038	Fair	17,900
Tool Design Drafter	007.261-022	Good	16,800

Occupational Personality Styles: Technical, Detail-oriented, Artistic

DPT Functions: Data = H   People = L   Things = H

GOE Work Group: Engineering Technology

Electrician

Electricians work on building sites and follow blueprints to install wiring in buildings. They plan and estimate contracts and materials, select and purchase materials, and install the wiring systems. Electricians may also work as maintenance electricians and keep electrical equipment in working order. Electricians normally work as independent contractors or for other contractors. In addition, maintenance electricians may be employed by industrial companies.

EDUCATIONAL REQUIREMENTS

Electricians may complete a two-year program leading to an Associate of Science degree. Most electricians work in apprenticeships for four years in programs sponsored by labor unions and trade councils.

COURSE REQUIREMENTS

AC/DC Electrical Theory
AC/DC Motors and Generators
Blueprint Reading
Construction Wiring Practices
Electrical Codes and Ordinances
Electrical Drafting and Design
Electrical Planning and
    Estimation

Industrial Control Systems
Mathematics
Motor and Generator Principles
Physics
Power Distribution Systems
Residential Wiring
Troubleshooting
    Procedures

RECOMMENDED HIGH SCHOOL COURSES

Drafting
Electrical Shop
English

Mathematics (including Algebra)
Physics
Wood Shop

CAREERS	D.O.T. NUMBERS	OUTLOOK	AVERAGE INITIAL SALARIES
Airplane Electrician	825.261-018	Excellent	$33,000
Airport Electrician	824.281-010	Good	26,700
Electric Distribution Checker	824.281-014	Excellent	20,500
Electrical Technician	003.161-010	Good	22,000
Electrician Supervisor	829.131-014	Excellent	35,600
Electrician, Wirer	829.684-014	Excellent	26,500
Motion-Picture/TV Electrician	824.137-010	Good	24,500
Powerhouse Electrician	820.261-014	Good	22,700
Substation Electrician	820.261-018	Good	22,700

Occupational Personality Styles: Technical, Detail-oriented

DPT Functions: Data = H   People = L   Things = H

GOE Work Groups: Crafts, Craft Technology

Electronics Repair

Electronics technicians diagnose and repair electrical and electronic equipment malfunctions. They may troubleshoot and repair televisions, radios, videocassette recorders, and other electronics equipment. Some technicians may sell, install, and service auto stereo systems, stereo sound systems, compact disc players, video disc players, and cellular car telephones. Some technicians will service short- and long-distance communications equipment. Other technicians will repair appliances such as refrigerators, clothes dryers, and microwave ovens. Employment opportunities exist in appliance stores, department stores, with equipment manufacturers, or as self-employed technicians.

EDUCATIONAL REQUIREMENTS

Electronics technicians normally complete a two-year program leading to an Associate of Applied Science degree in electronics technology. Positions requiring work on telecommunications equipment require an FCC Radio/Telephone License. Technicians may also take the Certified Electronics Technician (CET) examination.

COURSE REQUIREMENTS

AC and DC Electricity
AC and DC Electronics
Appliance Repair
Audio and RF Amplifiers
Audio Electronic Circuits
Electric Motor Repair

Electronic Communications Theory
Energy Management
Laser Theory
Microprocessor Applications
Television and Radio Theory
    and Troubleshooting Techniques

RECOMMENDED HIGH SCHOOL COURSES

Drafting
Electrical Shop
English

Mathematics
Physics

CAREERS	D.O.T. NUMBERS	OUTLOOK	AVERAGE INITIAL SALARIES
Automotive Electrician	825.281-022	Excellent	$18,500
Electric Meter Repairer	729.281-014	Fair	18,500
Electrical Appliance Repairer	723.381-010	Good	18,500
Electrical Appliance Servicer	827.261-010	Good	17,500
Electrical Instrument Repairer	729.281-026	Good	19,500
Electrical Repairer	829.261-018	Good	18,500
Electronic Motor Repairer	721.281-018	Good	19,900
Electronic Sales and Service Technician	828.251-010	Good	17,000
Radio Electrician	823.281-014	Good	16,000
Radio Mechanic	823.261-018	Fair	17,000
Telephone Maintenance Mechanic	822.281-018	Good	19,500

Occupational Personality Styles: Technical, Detail-oriented

DPT Functions: Data = H   People = L   Things = H

GOE Work Groups: Crafts, Craft Technology

Electronics Technology

Electronics technicians develop, test, manufacture, and service electronic equipment. They work from schematics created by engineers to build prototype equipment. Technicians may inspect and test electronic products and may assist engineers in solving production and quality control problems. Some technicians will work as electronic system testers and quality control technicians. Others may work as field service and technical representatives. Some technicians may also work as research technicians in assisting engineers in the development of new technology.

EDUCATIONAL REQUIREMENTS

Most electronics technicians complete a two-year program leading to an Associate of Applied Science degree. Technicians may also take the Certified Electronics Technician (CET) examination.

COURSE REQUIREMENTS

AC and DC Electrical Theory
Computer Arithmetic Systems
Computer Programming
Data Transmission Principles
Digital Electronics
Digital Troubleshooting
Electromagnetics
Electromechanical Systems
Electronic Controls

Electronic Design
Integrated Circuits
Linear Equations
Microprocessor Theory
Network Analysis
Schematic Drawing and
    Interpretation
Semiconductor Theory
Transient Analysis

RECOMMENDED HIGH SCHOOL COURSES

Computers
Drafting
Electrical Shop

English
Mathematics (3 years or more)
Physics

CAREERS	D.O.T. NUMBERS	OUTLOOK	AVERAGE INITIAL SALARIES
Electronics Systems Supervisor	828.161-010	Good	$27,000
Electronics Technician	003.161-014	Fair/Good	19,600
Plant Technician	822.281-030	Fair	21,000
Semiconductor Development Technician	003.161-018	Good	19,900
Sensor Specialist	378.382-010	Fair	18,000

Occupational Personality Styles:	Technical, Detail-oriented
DPT Functions:	Data = H People = L Things = H
GOE Work Groups:	Crafts, Craft Technology, Engineering Technology

Emergency Medical Technology

Emergency medical technicians (EMTs) travel to emergencies to assist sick or injured people. They evaluate patients' conditions and administer emergency care. They maintain this treatment until the patient is delivered to a hospital. EMTs work for police and fire departments, private ambulance companies, hospitals, and industrial companies.

EDUCATIONAL REQUIREMENTS

EMTs usually acquire training on a part-time basis through organizations such as the Red Cross. State certification is usually required. Training usually includes mandatory participation in ambulance and/or hospital emergency room activities.

COURSE REQUIREMENTS

Anatomy   Medical Terminology
Biology   Microbiology
Cardiopulmonary Resuscitation   Pharmacology
Emergency Medical Procedures   Physiology

RECOMMENDED HIGH SCHOOL COURSES

Biology   Health
Chemistry   Mathematics
English

CAREERS	D.O.T. NUMBERS	OUTLOOK	AVERAGE INITIAL SALARIES
Emergency Medical Services Coordinator	079.117-010	Good	$23,600
Emergency Medical Technician	079.374-010	Excellent	18,900

Occupational Personality Styles: Technical, Scientific, Serving

DPT Functions: Data = H   People = H   Things = H

GOE Work Groups: Laboratory Technology, Life Sciences, Medical Sciences

Engineering Technology

Engineering technicians assist engineers in planning and designing. They estimate costs, prepare materials specifications, and create engineering drawings. They may also assist contractors in scheduling activities and inspecting work. Employment opportunities may be found with engineering companies and government agencies.

EDUCATIONAL REQUIREMENTS

Engineering technicians normally complete a two-year program leading to an Associate of Science or an Associate of Applied Science degree. Typically there is not a universal engineering technology program; rather, a specific area is offered.

COURSE REQUIREMENTS

Calculus
Drafting
Materials Science
Mathematics (including
   Trigonometry)

Physics
Strength of Materials
Structural Engineering
Surveying Techniques

RECOMMENDED HIGH SCHOOL COURSES

Biology
Chemistry
Earth Science
English

Mathematics (including
   Trigonometry)
Physics

CAREERS	D.O.T. NUMBERS	OUTLOOK	AVERAGE INITIAL SALARIES
Chemical Engineer Technician	008.261-010	Excellent	$20,000
Chemistry Technologist	078.261-010	Good	25,500
Civil Engineer Technician	005.261-014	Excellent	18,900
Heat Transfer Technician	007.181-010	Good	19,300
Industrial Engineering Technician	012.267-010	Good	19,300
Laser Technician	019.261-034	Good	17,100
Mechanical Engineer Technician	007.161-026	Good/Exc.	23,600
Optomechanical Engineer Technician	007.161-030	Good	20,300
Test Technician	019.261-022	Fair	19,300

Occupational Personality Styles: Technical, Scientific

DPT Functions: Data = H   People = L   Things = H

GOE Work Group: Engineering Technology

Environmental Technology

Environmental technology professionals work in several areas related to pollution control. Solid-waste management technicians operate and maintain sanitation and public health facilities and waste treatment plants. Water systems technicians operate and maintain municipal water supply, purification, and distribution systems. Research technicians help engineers to develop new waste treatment and water sanitation processes. Public health technicians monitor industrial discharges, ground water purification, air quality, and water quality.

EDUCATIONAL REQUIREMENTS

Most environmental technicians complete a two-year program leading to an Associate of Science degree. Water and waste treatment plant operators may undergo training which may last several months. Apprenticeships are available in some areas of the country. In many municipalities, environmental technicians must be licensed or certified.

COURSE REQUIREMENTS

Solid-waste Management Technician

Environmental Microbiology
Industrial Waste
Landfills
Refuse Collection

Resource Recovery
Solid-Waste Management
Wastewater Operations

Water Systems Technicians

Aquatic Microbiology
Bacteriology
Culinary Water Treatment
Water Hydraulics

Water Purification
Water System Controls
Water Treatment

RECOMMENDED HIGH SCHOOL COURSES

Biology   English
Botany   Geology
Chemistry   Mathematics
Earth Science   Physics

CAREERS	D.O.T. NUMBERS	OUTLOOK	AVERAGE INITIAL SALARIES
Industrial Waste Inspector	168.267-054	Fair	$19,600
Pollution Control Technician	029.261-014	Fair	15,000
Radiation Monitor	199.167-010	Fair	17,500
Sanitarium	529.137-014	Good	19,000
Water Quality Tester	539.367-014	Fair	15,800

Occupational Personality Styles: Scientific, Serving

DPT Functions: Data = H   People = M   Things = M

GOE Work Group: Quality Control

Farm Management

Farm managers work in the area of livestock and crop management. They test and fertilize soils as needed and build irrigation and drainage systems. They work to stimulate crop improvements through fertilizer and weed and pest control. They plant forage crops for livestock and cut, dry, and store hay for feeding to cattle. Farm managers supervise the breeding, raising, and marketing of livestock. They may work on their own farm, or they may be hired to manage a farm owned by someone else. They may also be employed as agricultural agents, farm consultants, and extension agents.

EDUCATIONAL REQUIREMENTS

Farm managers usually complete a two-year program leading to an Associate of Science degree. Some schools may require internships on working farms.

COURSE REQUIREMENTS

Agricultural Accounting
Agricultural Laws
Agricultural Machinery
Agricultural Marketing
Agricultural Structures
Botany
Cattle Anatomy
Cattle Reproduction
Chemistry
Farm Management
Feedlot Management

Field Crop Production
Forage Crops
Irrigation and Drainage
Livestock Production
Mathematics
Pest Management
Practical Veterinary Skills
Soil Fertility
Weed Science
Welding

RECOMMENDED HIGH SCHOOL COURSES

Agriculture
Biology
Botany

Business
Earth Science
English

CAREERS	D.O.T. NUMBERS	OUTLOOK	AVERAGE INITIAL SALARIES
Cash Grain Farmer	401.161-010	Good	$19,000
Diversified Crop Farmer	407.161-010	Fair/Good	17,200
Farm Manager	186.167-034	Fair	22,600
Farmer	401.161-010	Good	17,300
Field Crop Farmer	404.161-010	Fair	17,500
Fruit and Nut Farmer	403.161-010	Good/Exc.	19,000
Vegetable Farmer	402.161-010	Fair/Good	17,500
Vine Crop Farmer	403.161-014	Fair	17,500

Occupational Personality Styles: Technical, Detail-oriented, Influencing

DPT Functions: Data = H   People = L   Things = H

GOE Work Groups: Life Sciences, Managerial Work: Plants and Animals

Fashion Design Technology

Fashion design technicians create original fashion styles by drawing sketches or draping mannequins. They may work as custom sewers or tailors. They measure clients for proper fit, cut fabrics, and sew clothing together. They may also make alterations as necessary. Fashion design technicians may also work as designers, pattern makers, or production managers. They may work in clothing stores, sewing shops, or tailor shops. They may also be self-employed or work for clothing manufacturers.

EDUCATIONAL REQUIREMENTS

Fashion design technicians normally complete a two-year program leading to an Associate of Science degree.

COURSE REQUIREMENTS

Fashion Designers

Clothing Construction
Elements of Design
Fashion Design
Fashion History
Fashion Merchandising

Fashion Sketching
Pattern Analysis
Pattern Making
Textile Dying and Printing

Custom Sewing/Tailoring

Children and Adult Clothing
Clothing Design
Creative Stitchery
Custom Sewing
Drapery Construction
Dress Design and Construction

Fabric Selection and Care
Fitting and Alterations
Hand Stitching
Marketing
Retailing
Tailoring

RECOMMENDED HIGH SCHOOL COURSES

Art
Business
Drafting
English

Fine Arts
Home Economics
Sewing

CAREERS	D.O.T. NUMBERS	OUTLOOK	AVERAGE INITIAL SALARIES
Cloth Designer	142.061-014	Fair	$16,200
Clothes Designer	142.061-018	Fair	18,300
Copyist, Garment	142.281-010	Fair	18,000
Displayer, Merchandise	298.081-010	Good	12,500
Fashion Artist	141.061-014	Fair/Good	21,200
Fashion Coordinator	185.157-010	Good	23,400
Fur Designer	142.081-014	Fair	22,000
Illustrator	141.061-022	Fair/Good	19,500

Occupational Personality Styles: Artistic, Conventional, Social

DPT Functions: Data = M   People = H   Things = H

GOE Work Group: Craft Technology, Visual Arts

Fashion Merchandising

Fashion merchandisers design, buy, and sell fashion merchandise. They select products, set pricing guidelines, develop fashion displays, and supply retail clothing products to the public. They may be employed as bridal consultants, copywriters, display artists, fashion promoters, or fashion consultants. Employment opportunities exist with department stores or boutiques, advertising agencies, modeling agencies, and clothing companies.

EDUCATIONAL REQUIREMENTS

Fashion merchandisers normally complete a two-year program leading to an Associate of Science degree.

COURSE REQUIREMENTS

Accounting
Advertising
Art
Business Communications
Business Management
Business Mathematics
Display Techniques
Drawing
English
Fashion Analysis

Fashion Promotion
Fashion Show Production
Marketing
Principles of Merchandising
Psychology
Retail Buying
Retailing
Sales
Textiles

RECOMMENDED HIGH SCHOOL COURSES

Art
Business
Drafting
English

Home Economics
Mathematics
Sewing

CAREERS	D.O.T. NUMBERS	OUTLOOK	AVERAGE INITIAL SALARIES
Buyer	162.157-018	Good/Exc.	$23,000
Cloth Designer	142.061-014	Fair	16,200
Displayer, Merchandise	298.081-010	Good	12,500
Fashion Consultant	096.121-014	Good	24,000
Fashion Coordinator	185.157-010	Good	23,400
Fashion Designer	142.061-018	Fair	19,900
Fashion Stylist	185.157-010	Fair	17,500
Illustrator	141.061-022	Fair/Good	19,500

Occupational Personality Styles: Influencing, Artistic

DPT Functions: Data = H   People = L   Things = H

GOE Work Groups: General Sales, Sales Technology, Visual Arts

Fire Science

Firefighters operate complex firefighting equipment in order to extinguish fires. They may enter buildings in search of trapped people. Firefighters may also work as building inspectors, arson investigators, and in public fire-safety training. Fire science technicians may work for insurance companies or municipal firefighting departments.

EDUCATIONAL REQUIREMENTS

Firefighters usually must pass physical and written examinations to enter firefighting organizations. These organizations usually administer the type of training needed. In some local areas of the country, licensing may be required. Firefighters must continually undergo refresher courses and new training.

COURSE REQUIREMENTS

Building Construction
Fire Apparatus
Fire Codes and Ordinances
Fire Ground Hydraulics
Fire Investigation
Fire Prevention
Fire Protection Systems

Firefighting Fundamentals
Firefighting Water Supplies
First Aid
Hazardous Materials
Rescue Operations
Technical Mathematics

RECOMMENDED HIGH SCHOOL COURSES

Chemistry
Electrical Shop
English

Mathematics
Metal Shop
Wood Shop

CAREERS	D.O.T. NUMBERS	OUTLOOK	AVERAGE INITIAL SALARIES
Fire Assistant	169.167-022	Fair	$22,300
Fire Captain	373.134-010	Good	28,000
Fire Chief	373.117-010	Good	33,600
Fire Chief Aide	373.363-010	Poor	15,500
Fire Control Technician	632.261-014	Fair	18,500
Fire Equipment Inspector	739.484-014	Fair	17,900
Fire Inspector	373.267-010	Good	25,600
Fire Investigator	373.267-010	Good	25,600

Occupational Personality Styles: Technical, Scientific

DPT Functions: Data = H   People = L   Things = H

GOE Work Groups: Safety and Law Enforcement, Security Services

Food Service

Food service professionals plan menus, purchase food supplies, and supervise food preparation. They ensure that meals are well prepared, properly cooked, and attractively presented. They are skilled in food cost control, sanitation, and food management. Some food service professionals work as short-order cooks or bakers. Employment opportunities exist in restaurants, hospitals, schools, hotels and catering firms, and airline, railroad, and steamship companies.

EDUCATIONAL REQUIREMENTS

Many food service professionals complete a two-year program leading to an Associate of Science degree. Chefs and bakers usually attend cooking schools and are normally required to work for one year or more as apprentices. Many chefs get their training in the military.

COURSE REQUIREMENTS

Cafeteria Management
Cake Decorating
Catering
Cost Estimating
Dietetics
Fast-food Cooking
Food Management
Food Purchasing

Gourmet Cooking
Government Regulations
Institutional Cooking
Kitchen Management
Meat Planning
Menu Cutting
Nutrition
Sanitation

RECOMMENDED HIGH SCHOOL COURSES

Accounting
Bookkeeping
Business Mathematics
Chemistry

English
Health
Home Economics

The Career Connection for Technical Education

CAREERS	D.O.T. NUMBERS	OUTLOOK	AVERAGE INITIAL SALARIES
Baker	313.381-010	Good	$18,000
Chef	313.131-014	Good	19,200
Food and Beverage Analyst	310.267-010	Fair	19,900
Food and Beverage Controller	216.362-022	Fair	18,500
Food Concession Manager	185.167-022	Excellent	17,500
Food Service Supervisor	211.137-014	Excellent	23,000
Sous Chef	313.131-026	Fair	23,000

Occupational Personality Styles: Technical, Detail-oriented

DPT Functions: Data = M   People = M   Things = M

GOE Work Groups: Customer Services, General Sales, Hospitality Services

Graphic Arts

Graphic artists find career opportunities in advertising agencies and promotion programs. They create the visual effects for brochures, prospectus material, billboards, and other advertising functions. Not all professionals are artists, but they design visual materials through format and color combinations. Graphic artists must balance creativity with time deadlines.

EDUCATIONAL REQUIREMENTS

This is a two-year program leading to an Associate of Science degree.

COURSE REQUIREMENTS

Advertising Design
Advertising Theory
Color Theory and Practice
Corporate Identity Design
Illustration

Packaging Design
Publication Design
Two/Three-Dimensional Design
Visual Communications

RECOMMENDED HIGH SCHOOL COURSES

Art
Drafting

English
Graphic Arts

CAREERS	D.O.T. NUMBERS	OUTLOOK	AVERAGE INITIAL SALARIES
Advertising Designer	247.387-010	Good	$18,200
Copy Artist	141.061-022	Good	17,900
Graphic Artist	141.061-022	Good	18,200
Layout Designer	141.061-018	Good	18,200

Occupational Personality Styles: Artistic, Detail-oriented

DPT Functions: Data = H   People = M   Things = H

GOE Work Groups: Craft Arts, Visual Arts

Heating, Ventilation, and Air Conditioning (HVAC) Technology

HVAC technicians perform many tasks related to the installation and maintenance of heating, ventilation, and air conditioning systems. Technicians may calculate heating and cooling needs and capacities and help engineers to design, manufacture, and install climate control equipment. They work on systems that modify the temperature, humidity, and air quality of buildings. They install heating, cooling, and ventilation units; fans; ducts; and pumps. After installing HVAC systems, technicians test the systems for compliance with specifications. They may also diagnose and repair malfunctioning equipment. HVAC technicians may also work as sales representatives or service technicians. Employment opportunities may be found with utility companies, air conditioning contractors, or as self-employed contractors.

EDUCATIONAL REQUIREMENTS

HVAC technicians normally complete a two-year program that leads to an Associate of Science degree or an Associate of Applied Science degree. An apprenticeship of up to five years may be substituted for a degree.

COURSE REQUIREMENTS

AC and DC Electrical Theory	Pneumatics
Basic Heating and Cooling	Psychrometry
Blueprint Reading	Refrigeration Theory
Drafting	Solar Energy
Electronic Control Systems	Strength of Materials
Heat Gain Theory	Technical Mathematics
Physics	Thermodynamics
Piping Practices	Welding

RECOMMENDED HIGH SCHOOL COURSES

Chemistry
Drafting
Electrical Shop
English

Industrial Arts
Mathematics (including Algebra)
Metal Shop
Physics

CAREERS	D.O.T. NUMBERS	OUTLOOK	AVERAGE INITIAL SALARIES
Air-Conditioning Installer	637.687-010	Good	$18,000
Air-Conditioning Mechanic	620.281-010	Good	21,100
Heating Technician	007.181-010	Good	18,000
Refrigeration Mechanic	637.261-026	Good	21,100
Refrigeration Repairer	637.381-014	Good	20,000

Occupational Personality Styles: Technical, Detail-oriented

DPT Functions: Data = H   People = M   Things = H

GOE Work Groups: Craft Technology, Production Work

Heavy-Equipment Operations

Heavy-equipment operators run machines used to move earth and materials, erect steel beams and guides, and other associated tasks in construction. They may operate bulldozers, cranes, earth movers, or paving machines. They operate excavating equipment and prepare highway beds for surfacing. They make minor repairs on heavy equipment and may have additional skills in welding, mechanics, or surveying. Heavy-equipment operators, also known as operating engineers, normally work for construction contractors.

EDUCATIONAL REQUIREMENTS

Heavy-equipment operators may attend a trade school for up to one year to receive a certificate of completion. Operators may also obtain training through apprenticeships. Many heavy-equipment operators receive their training in the military.

COURSE REQUIREMENTS

Diesel Electrical Systems
Diesel Engine Theory
Driving
First Aid
Heavy-Equipment Maintenance
Heavy-Equipment Operation and
   Skill Development
Hydraulics
Rigging
Surveying
Technical Mathematics
Welding

RECOMMENDED HIGH SCHOOL COURSES

Auto Shop
Driver Education
Earth Science
English
Mathematics
Physics

CAREERS	D.O.T. NUMBERS	OUTLOOK	AVERAGE INITIAL SALARIES
Bulldozer Operator	850.683-010	Good	$22,100
Core-drill Operator	930.382-014	Fair	20,600
Crane Crew Operator	921.133-010	Good	27,400
Derrick Operator	921.663-022	Good	26,600
Dragline Operator	850.683-018	Fair	25,100
Dredge Operator	850.663-010	Fair	23,100
Grader (Patrol) Operator	850.663-022	Good	25,000
Loading Machine Operator	932.683-014	Fair	19,500
Pneumatic Hoist Operator	921.663-046	Fair	23,900
Power Shovel Operator	850.683-030	Good	30,600
Rock Drill Operator	850.683-034	Fair	23,100
Stevedore	911.663-014	Fair	34,000

Occupational Personality Style: Technical

DPT Functions: Data = L   People = L   Things = H

GOE Work Group: Land and Water Vehicle Operation

Hotel Management

Hotel managers oversee hotel reservations and rentals, housekeeping, and food and beverage operations. They develop advertising, publicity, and personnel policies. Hotel managers plan dining room, bar, and banquet operations. They manage food service operations, accounting, security, and maintenance operations. They often begin as reservation clerks and work their way up into management positions. Employment opportunities exist with independent motels and with hotel/motel chains.

EDUCATIONAL REQUIREMENTS

Hotel managers normally complete a two-year program leading to an Associate of Science degree.

COURSE REQUIREMENTS

Advertising
Banquet Promotion
Facility Maintenance
Food Preparation

Hotel Desk Procedures
Hotel/Motel Management
Public Speaking
Quantity Food Production

RECOMMENDED HIGH SCHOOL COURSES

Accounting
Bookkeeping
Business Law
Business Mathematics
Computer Operations
English

Fine Arts
Health
Home Economics
Psychology
Sociology

CAREERS	D.O.T. NUMBERS	OUTLOOK	AVERAGE INITIAL SALARIES
Convention Manager	187.167-078	Excellent	$21,900
Dude Ranch Manager	187.167-094	Good	20,000
Front Office Manager	187.137-018	Good	21,000
Hotel/Motel Manager	187.117-038	Excellent	25,300
Hotel, Recreation Manager	187.167-122	Fair	18,200
Lodging Facility Manager	320.137-014	Excellent	20,000

Occupational Personality Styles: Influencing, Serving

DPT Functions: Data = H   People = H   Things = L

GOE Work Groups: Business Management, Hospitality Services

Information Technology and Data Processing

Information technicians enter data into computer systems and operate computers and associated equipment. They operate and apply software systems. Some technicians design systems for processing information, write instructions, and translate them into machine-readable format. Other technicians may design, code, test, and implement commercial information-gathering systems. Information technicians may work as data entry operators, programmers, computer operators, systems analysts, or data control clerks. Employment opportunities exist in banks, insurance companies, businesses, and government agencies.

EDUCATIONAL REQUIREMENTS

Data processing technicians normally complete a one or two-year program leading to an Associate of Applied Science degree. Information technicians normally complete a two-year program leading to an Associate of Science degree.

COURSE REQUIREMENTS

Accounting	Economics
Assembly Computer Language	English
Basic Computer Language	Fortran Computer Language
Business Law	Information Management
Business Mathematics	Marketing
Cobol Computer Language	Pascal Computer Language
College Algebra	Programming
Computer Operations	Statistics
Data Base Management	Word Processing
Data Management	Writing Programs
Data Processing	

RECOMMENDED HIGH SCHOOL COURSES

Accounting
Business Mathematics
Computer Operations

Data Processing
English
Typing/Word Processing

CAREERS	D.O.T. NUMBERS	OUTLOOK	AVERAGE INITIAL SALARIES
Administrative Assistant	169.167-010	Excellent	$18,100
Clerk-Typist	203.362-010	Good	14,000
Data Entry Clerk	203.582-054	Excellent	18,000
Data Typist	203.582-054	Good	14,000
Executive Secretary	189.117-010	Excellent	20,000
Legal Secretary	201.362-010	Excellent	16,500
Medical Secretary	079.367-018	Excellent	17,000
Receptionist	237.367-038	Good	13,700
School Secretary	201.362-022	Poor	15,600
Secretary	201.362-030	Excellent	16,600
Stenographer	202.362-014	Poor	16,100
Terminal Operator	203.362-014	Excellent	14,000
Transcribing Machine Operator	203.582-058	Excellent	14,000
Typist	203.582-066	Good	14,000
Word Processing Supervisor	203.137-010	Excellent	22,900

Occupational Personality Style: Detail-oriented

DPT Functions: Data = H   People = M   Things = L

GOE Work Groups: Administrative Detail, Clerical Machine Operation, Clerical Handling

Interior Design

Interior designers make residential, commercial, and public areas more attractive and functional. They plan layouts, color schemes, and furnishings; purchase furnishings; and supervise workers in the implementation of the designs. Interior designers may also work as salespeople, designers, illustrators, or manufacturer representatives. They may be employed by interior-design companies, department stores, or architectural companies.

EDUCATIONAL REQUIREMENTS

Interior designers may complete a two-year program leading to an Associate of Science degree.

COURSE REQUIREMENTS

Architecture	Drawing
Art History	Fabric Design
Business Procedures	Historical Furnishings
Color Theory	Interior Design
Display Design	Lighting
Drafting	Photography
Draperies	Space Planning

RECOMMENDED HIGH SCHOOL COURSES

Art	Fine Arts
Drafting	Mathematics
English	Psychology

CAREERS	D.O.T. NUMBERS	OUTLOOK	AVERAGE INITIAL SALARIES
Display Designer	142.051-014	Fair	$16,000
Displayer, Merchandise	298.081-010	Good	12,500
Furniture Salesperson	270.357-030	Good	16,500
Graphic Designer	141.067-018	Good	18,200
Interior Designer	142.051-014	Good	17,900

Occupational Personality Styles: Artistic, Detail-oriented

DPT Functions: Data = H   People = M   Things = H

GOE Work Groups: Craft Arts, Promotion, Visual Arts

Jewelry Design and Metal Smithing

Jewelry designers create original designs and work gemstones, gold, silver, and other materials into rings, necklaces, and other types of jewelry. They usually work for a jewelry company or own their own business.

EDUCATIONAL REQUIREMENTS

Jewelry designers and metal smiths are largely self-taught. However, they may attend trade school for up to one year to receive a certificate of completion.

COURSE REQUIREMENTS

Advertising
Art
Business Management
Design

Lapidary Techniques
Marketing
Metallurgy
Salesmanship

RECOMMENDED HIGH SCHOOL COURSES

Art
Crafts
Drafting
Earth Science

English
Industrial Arts
Metal Shop
Wood Shop

CAREERS	D.O.T. NUMBERS	OUTLOOK	AVERAGE INITIAL SALARIES
Diamond Finisher	770.387-022	Fair	$25,300
Gem Cutter	770.281-014	Good	22,300
Jeweler	700.281-010	Good	20,000
Jewelry Model Maker	709.381-022	Fair	22,500
Pearl Restorer	735.381-014	Poor	18,900
Silversmith	700.281-022	Good	22,900
Stone Setter	700.281-014	Fair	21,000

Occupational Personality Styles: Technical, Artistic

DPT Functions: Data = M   People = L   Things = H

GOE Work Groups: Craft Arts, Craft Technology, Visual Arts

Journalism

Journalists search out news and write newspaper and magazine stories about newsworthy events. Journalists may also work in radio or television newsgathering. Journalists are typically assigned areas of news to cover. Examples include sports, crime, lifestyles, and personals. They may work as editors on newspapers or magazines, or as journalism technicians.

EDUCATIONAL REQUIREMENTS

Journalists and journalism technicians normally complete a two-year program leading to an Associate of Science degree.

COURSE REQUIREMENTS

Advertising
Business Law
English
History
Mass Communications
Mechanics and Expressions

Natural Sciences
News Reporting
Newswriting
Photography
Printing Processes
Public Speaking

RECOMMENDED HIGH SCHOOL COURSES

Business Law
English
History
Journalism

Shorthand
Speech
Typing/Word Processing

CAREERS	D.O.T. NUMBERS	OUTLOOK	AVERAGE INITIAL SALARIES
Assignment Editor	132.132-010	Good	$19,900
Editorial Assistant	132.267-014	Fair	16,500
Newswriter	131.262-014	Good	15,900
Reporter	131.262-018	Excellent	18,800
Technical Writer	131.267-026	Good	19,300

Occupational Personality Styles: Social, Influencing

DPT Functions: Data = H   People = L   Things = L

GOE Work Groups: Communications, Literary Arts

Law Enforcement

Law enforcement professionals may work in many fields. Some professionals will work on state, county, and local police forces as patrolmen, detectives, or administrators. Other professionals may work for private security companies as guards, bodyguards, and detectives. Many businesses now have their own security people who safeguard company property and employees. Some law enforcement professionals may work as private detectives.

EDUCATIONAL REQUIREMENTS

Some law enforcement professionals may complete a two-year program leading to an Associate of Science degree. State, county, and local law enforcement professionals attend specialized training and must normally undergo further training throughout their careers. Private agency professionals and private detectives normally must obtain state licensing. All professionals who wish to carry firearms must receive special permits to do so.

COURSE REQUIREMENTS

Abnormal Psychology
Civil and Business Law
Criminal Investigation
Criminal Justice
Criminal Law
Drug Abuse
Interpersonal Communications

Listening Skills
Patrol Procedure
Psychology
Public Speaking
Sociology
Traffic and Vehicle Codes

RECOMMENDED HIGH SCHOOL COURSES

Biology
Business Law
Chemistry
English

Health
Psychology
Sociology
Speech

CAREERS	D.O.T. NUMBERS	OUTLOOK	AVERAGE INITIAL SALARIES
Correction Officer	372.667-018	Excellent	$19,000
Deputy Sheriff	377.167-010	Excellent	19,000
Detective	375.267-010	Excellent	23,900
Police Captain	375.167-034	Excellent	37,100
Police Chief	375.117-010	Excellent	39,900
Police Inspector	375.267-026	Excellent	34,600
Police Officer	375.263-014	Excellent	19,000
Private Investigator	376.267-018	Excellent	22,600
State-highway Patrol Officer	375.263-018	Excellent	23,600

Occupational Personality Styles: Technical, Detail-oriented

DPT Functions: Data = H   People = L   Things = L

GOE Work Groups: Safety and Law Enforcement, Security Services

Library–Media Technology

Library technicians support professional librarians in libraries, information centers, and corporate libraries. They catalog books, films, and other library supplies; maintain library records systems; and perform other library or media center jobs as necessary.

EDUCATIONAL REQUIREMENTS

Library technicians normally complete a two-year program leading to an Associate of Science degree.

COURSE REQUIREMENTS

Algebra
Business Communications
Cataloging
English
Library Procedures
Literature

Media Materials
Public Speaking
Technical Services
Typing/Word Processing
Writing

RECOMMENDED HIGH SCHOOL COURSES

Computer Operations
English
Fine Arts
History
Humanities

Journalism
Literature
Mathematics
Printing Technology
Typing/Word Processing

CAREERS	D.O.T. NUMBERS	OUTLOOK	AVERAGE INITIAL SALARIES
Audiovisual Librarian	100.167-010	Fair	$15,900
Bookmobile Librarian	100.167-014	Fair	14,500
Classifier	100.367-014	Fair	14,500
Library Assistant	249.367-046	Fair	13,300
Music Librarian	100.367-022	Fair	15,900
School Librarian/Media	100.167-030	Good/Exc.	15,900

Occupational Personality Styles: Detail-oriented, Technical, Serving

DPT Functions: Data = H   People = M   Things = L

GOE Work Group: Educational and Library Services

Machine Technology

Machinists work from blueprints to select, set up, and operate production metal working machines to machine metal parts. They may also use heat treating techniques if required. They operate a variety of machining and tool and die equipment to produce parts to precise specifications.

EDUCATIONAL REQUIREMENTS

Machinists may complete a two-year program leading to an Associate of Science degree. However, most machinists develop their skills in apprenticeships lasting from eighteen months to four years. Apprentice programs are normally controlled by labor unions or trade councils, but manufacturing companies often offer apprenticeships as well.

COURSE REQUIREMENTS

Blueprint Reading
Drafting
Foundry
Lathe Operations
Machine Shop Theory and
    Practice
Manufacturing Processes
Mathematics

Metallurgy
Metal Working
Numerical Control Systems
Principles of Machined Tools
Tool and Die Design
Vertical and Horizontal Mill
    Operations

RECOMMENDED HIGH SCHOOL COURSES

Drafting
English
Industrial Arts

Mathematics (2 years or more)
Metal Shop
Physics

CAREERS	D.O.T. NUMBERS	OUTLOOK	AVERAGE INITIAL SALARIES
Automotive Machinist	600.280-034	Excellent	$26,900
Machine Set-up Operator	600.380-018	Excellent	18,200
Machinist Apprentice	600.280-260	Excellent	18,200
Machinist, First Class	600.280-022	Excellent	19,900
Patternmaker	600.280-050	Good	19,000
Patternmaker Apprentice	600.280-046	Poor	15,800
Tool Setter	615.130-010	Excellent	18,200

Occupational Personality Style: Technical

DPT Functions: Data = H   People = L   Things = H

GOE Work Groups: Craft Technology, Managerial Work: Mechanical

Manufacturing Technology

Manufacturing technicians assist engineers in developing, designing, and planning the production of industrial and consumer goods. They draw and design parts and products from engineers' specifications. They may also analyze and design processing equipment and may supervise production operations. Manufacturing technicians may also assist engineers in solving production and quality-control problems. They also work as production planners, engineering aides, and tool and die designers. Technicians normally work for manufacturing companies.

EDUCATIONAL REQUIREMENTS

Manufacturing technicians normally complete a two-year program leading to an Associate of Science or an Associate of Applied Science degree. Continuing through a bachelor degree and training on computer-aided design equipment enlarges job market possibilities.

COURSE REQUIREMENTS

AC and DC Electricity	Manufacturing Analysis
Blueprint Reading	Manufacturing Automation
Chemistry	Manufacturing Processes
Drafting	Mathematics (including Calculus)
Engineering Materials	Metallurgy
English	Numerical Control Systems
Foundry	Pneumatics
Hydraulics	Production Planning
Machine Shop Theory	Tool Design
Machine Tool Operations	Welding

RECOMMENDED HIGH SCHOOL COURSES

Chemistry	Industrial Arts
Computer Operations	Mathematics (2 years or more)
Drafting	Metal Shop
Electrical Shop	Physics
English	

CAREERS	D.O.T. NUMBERS	OUTLOOK	AVERAGE INITIAL SALARIES
Die Designer	007.161-010	Good	$28,000
Die Designer Apprentice	007.161-014	Good	16,000
Die Drawing Checker	007.167-010	Excellent	16,000
Materials Science Technician	029.081-024	Good	17,000
Quality Control Technician	012.261-014	Good	17,500
Tool Designer	007.061-026	Good	28,000
Tool Designer Apprentice	007.061-030	Good	16,000

Occupational Personality Style: Technical

DPT Functions: Data = H   People = L   Things = H

GOE Work Groups: Craft Technology, Managerial Work: Mechanical

Mechanical Technology

Mechanical technicians assist engineers in designing products. They work out manufacturing procedures, material selection and costs, and production schedules. Mechanical technicians may operate machining equipment and supervise machining operations. Mechanical technicians may also work as equipment sales representatives, technical representatives, or service technicians. Employment opportunities are found in most industries.

EDUCATIONAL REQUIREMENTS

Mechanical technicians normally complete a two-year program leading to an Associate of Science degree or an Associate of Applied Science degree.

COURSE REQUIREMENTS

Blueprint Reading
Computer-Aided Design
Computerized Numerical Control
Drafting
Hydraulics
Machine Tool Operation

Materials Science
Mathematics (including Calculus)
Physics
Pneumatics
Production Engineering
Strength of Materials

RECOMMENDED HIGH SCHOOL COURSES

Chemistry
Drafting
English
Industrial Arts

Mathematics (3 years or more)
Metal Shop
Physics

CAREERS	D.O.T. NUMBERS	OUTLOOK	AVERAGE INITIAL SALARIES
Industrial Mechanics Salesperson	274.357-038	Good	$17,000
Machine Shop Supervisor	609.130-010	Good	27,500
Manager, Customer Technical Services	189.117-018	Good	19,300
Mechanical Technician	600.280-010	Good	17,800
Quality Control Technician	012.261-014	Good	17,500

Occupational Personality Style: Technical

DPT Functions: Data = H   People = L   Things = H

GOE Work Groups: Craft Technology, Managerial Work: Mechanical

Medical Assistant

Medical assistants help doctors treat patients. They help doctors perform clinical and administrative tasks, maintain patient records, handle correspondence, schedule appointments, and prepare billing statements. Medical assistants take and record patient weights and vital signs, and perform laboratory tests. They administer electrocardiographs, obtain blood samples, and apply bandages. They may also assist physicians in minor surgical procedures and other treatments. Medical assistants may find employment in clinics, hospitals, medical laboratories, and doctors' offices.

EDUCATIONAL REQUIREMENTS

Medical assistants normally complete a two-year program leading to an Associate of Science degree. Many health organizations prefer that job candidates successfully complete the national Certified Medical Assistant (CMA) examination and certification.

COURSE REQUIREMENTS

Anatomy
Biology
Business Communications
Clinical Procedures
Electrocardiography
Emergency Medical Procedures
English
Hematology
Medical Office Procedures
Medical Terminology
Medical Transcription
Microbiology
Pharmacology
Psychology
Public Speaking
Radiology
Typing
Urinalysis
Word Processing

RECOMMENDED HIGH SCHOOL COURSES

Biology
Chemistry
English
Health
Mathematics (2 years or more)
Psychology

The Career Connection for Technical Education

CAREERS	D.O.T. NUMBERS	OUTLOOK	AVERAGE INITIAL SALARIES
Medical Assistant	079.362-010	Excellent	$17,100
Orthopedic Assistant	078.664-010	Excellent	17,100
Podiatrist Assistant	079.374-018	Excellent	17,100

Occupational Personality Styles: Scientific, Detail-oriented, Serving

DPT Functions: Data = M   People = M   Things = H

GOE Work Groups: Clerical Handling, Medical Sciences

Medical–Dental Secretary

Medical and dental secretaries make patient appointments, schedule patient tests and hospital admissions, and maintain patient records. They may take health histories from patients. Secretaries also handle insurance forms, patient billing, bookkeeping, and correspondence. Medical and dental secretaries may find employment in doctors' or dentists' offices, clinics, hospitals, and insurance companies.

EDUCATIONAL REQUIREMENTS

Many medical and dental secretaries progress into the field from other secretarial positions. However, some secretaries may complete a two-year program leading to an Associate of Science degree. Some schools require an internship of up to four months.

COURSE REQUIREMENTS

Accounting
Bookkeeping
Cardiopulmonary Resuscitation
Emergency Medical Skills
Insurance
Medical Ethics
Medical Office Procedures

Medical Records Management
Medical Terminology
Public Speaking
Transcription
Typing
Word Processing

RECOMMENDED HIGH SCHOOL COURSES

Biology
Bookkeeping
Computer Operations
English
Health

Mathematics
Psychology
Shorthand
Typing
Word Processing

CAREERS	D.O.T. NUMBERS	OUTLOOK	AVERAGE INITIAL SALARIES
Dental Secretary	201.362-014	Excellent	$17,000
Medical Secretary	079.367-018	Excellent	17,000

Occupational Personality Styles: Technical, Serving

DPT Functions: Data = M   People = L   Things = M

GOE Work Groups: Clerical Handling, Contracts and Claims, Mathematical Detail

Medical Technology

Medical technicians perform chemical, microbiologic, and microscopic tests on patient specimens. They collect the specimens and examine and analyze the test results. They may prepare slides and isolate chemical components. Medical technicians write reports based upon their tests and submit the reports to physicians for diagnostic study. Medical technicians may specialize in such fields as microbiology, blood gas, hematology, and electrocardiography. Employment opportunities may be found in hospitals, clinics, doctors' offices, and police crime laboratories.

EDUCATIONAL REQUIREMENTS

Medical technicians normally complete training programs lasting from a few weeks to several months and receive a certificate of completion. Some medical technicians may complete a two-year program leading to an Associate of Science degree.

COURSE REQUIREMENTS

Anatomy
Biology
Chemistry
Hematology
Medical Terminology

Microbiology
Pharmacology
Physiology
Radiology
Urinalysis

RECOMMENDED HIGH SCHOOL COURSES

Biology
Chemistry
English

Health
Mathematics

CAREERS	D.O.T. NUMBERS	OUTLOOK	AVERAGE INITIAL SALARIES
Chemistry Technologist	078.261-010	Good	$25,500
Chief Medical Technologist	078.161-010	Excellent	32,500
Cytotechnologist	078.281-010	Excellent	20,000
Medical Technologist	078.261-038	Excellent	20,100
Microbiology Technologist	078.261-014	Excellent	21,200
Supervisory Medical Technologist	078.261.038	Excellent	29,000
Tissue Technologist	078.361-030	Excellent	21,200

Occupational Personality Styles: Technical, Scientific

DPT Functions: Data = H   People = L   Things = H

GOE Work Groups: Laboratory Technology, Life Sciences, Medical Sciences

Nurse's Aide

Nurse's aides make patients comfortable by providing basic care. They answer patient calls; serve meals; feed, bathe, and dress patients; and change bed linens. They may also take patient temperatures, give massages, and set up medical equipment. Nurse's aides may find employment opportunities in hospitals, nursing homes, and alternative health-care facilities.

EDUCATIONAL REQUIREMENTS

Nurse's aides normally complete a course of study that may last several weeks and includes internship work in patient-care settings.

COURSE REQUIREMENTS

Anatomy   Patient Care Techniques
Biology   Physiology
Medical Terminology

RECOMMENDED HIGH SCHOOL COURSES

Biology   Health
Chemistry   Psychology
English

CAREER	D.O.T. NUMBER	OUTLOOK	AVERAGE INITIAL SALARY
Nurse's Aide	355.674-014	Excellent	$15,300

Occupational Personality Style: Serving

DPT Functions: Data = L   People = L   Things = H

GOE Work Group: Hospitality Services

Nursing, Licensed Practical

Licensed practical nurses assist in the care and treatment of patients. They take temperatures and blood pressures, change dressings, and administer medication. Licensed practical nurses assist in examining patients and try to establish friendly relationships with patients and their families. They bring care and comfort to people who need health care, and assess, implement, and evaluate that care based on physical and psychological data. Licensed Practical Nurses (LPNs) may also be called Licensed Vocational Nurses (LVNs). Employment opportunities exist in hospitals, nursing homes, clinics, and alternative health-care facilities.

EDUCATIONAL REQUIREMENTS

Licensed practical nurses complete training that normally lasts several months, including internship work in health-care facilities. Before being hired, licensed practical nurses must pass the State Practical Nursing (SPN) examination.

COURSE REQUIREMENTS

Anatomy	Obstetrical Nursing
Maternity Care	Pediatrics
Medical Ethics	Pharmacology
Medical Terminology	Physiology
Microbiology	Psychiatric Nursing
Nursing Theory	Psychology
Nutrition	Surgical Nursing

RECOMMENDED HIGH SCHOOL COURSES

Biology	Health
Chemistry	Mathematics
English	Psychology

CAREER	D.O.T. NUMBER	OUTLOOK	AVERAGE INITIAL SALARY
Licensed Practical Nurse	079.374-014	Excellent	$16,200

Occupational Personality Styles:	Serving, Scientific
DPT Functions:	Data = H People = H Things = H
GOE Work Groups:	Life Sciences, Nursing, Therapy, and Specialized Teaching Services

Paralegal Services

Legal assistants assist attorneys in case research, document preparation, compiling client histories, and investigations. They research and prepare legal briefs for attorneys, and write personal and legal correspondence. They may also act as office managers for law offices. Legal assistants may also be known as paralegals. They normally are employed in law offices, legal-aid offices, courts, banks, insurance companies, and corporations.

EDUCATIONAL REQUIREMENTS

Legal assistants normally complete a two-year program leading to an Associate of Science degree. Some schools offer a one-year certificate of completion program.

COURSE REQUIREMENTS

Business Communications	Family Law
Business Law	Law Office Management
Civil Trial Practice	Legal Research
County Clerk Procedures	Probates and Estates
Criminal Law	Real Estate

RECOMMENDED HIGH SCHOOL COURSES

Accounting	Mathematics
Business Law	Shorthand
English	Typing
Latin	Word Processing

CAREER	D.O.T. NUMBER	OUTLOOK	AVERAGE INITIAL SALARY
Paralegal	119.267-026	Excellent	$21,400

Occupational Personality Style: Detail-oriented

DPT Functions: Data = H People = L Things = L

GOE Work Groups: Clerical Handling, Contracts and Claims, Law

Photography

Photographers work in many different environments to photograph people, places, and objects. Photographers usually specialize in fields of photography. Portrait photographers specialize in portraits, weddings, and other formal photography. Photojournalists may work for newspapers or magazines. They add interest and depth to news stories through photographs. Commercial photographers may work as independents or for advertising agencies. They photograph commercial products to be used in advertising displays.

EDUCATIONAL REQUIREMENTS

Many photographers are self-taught. Some photographers complete programs lasting from several weeks to a year and receive a certificate of completion. Some photographers complete a two-year program leading to an Associate of Science degree.

COURSE REQUIREMENTS

Art
Black/White Photographs
Chemistry
Colored Photographs
Commercial Photographic
    Techniques
Darkroom Techniques

Design and Composition
English
Photo Retouching
Photographic Materials
Print Enhancement
Studio Methods

RECOMMENDED HIGH SCHOOL COURSES

Art
Chemistry
English

Mathematics
Photography

CAREERS	D.O.T. NUMBERS	OUTLOOK	AVERAGE INITIAL SALARIES
Aerial Photographer	143.062-014	Fair	$18,000
Finish Photographer	143.382-014	Good	24,200
Lithographic Photographer	972.382-014	Excellent	29,100
Motion Picture Photographer	143.062-022	Excellent	28,600
Photographer	143.062-030	Good	21,800
Photojournalist	143.062-034	Fair	21,000
Scientific Photographer	143.062-026	Fair	21,300
Still Photographer	143.062-030	Fair	21,300

Occupational Personality Styles: Artistic, Technical, Scientific

DPT Functions: Data = H   People = M   Things = M

GOE Work Group: Visual Arts

Plastics Technology

Plastics technicians manufacture, extrude, and mold plastics for use in engineering applications. They assist design engineers in developing product molds and assist process engineers in developing optimum processing and parameters. Plastics technicians may be employed as research technicians, product development specialists, technical representatives, or marketing representatives. Employment opportunities may be found in research laboratories, plastics manufacturing companies, and plastics molding firms.

EDUCATIONAL REQUIREMENTS

Plastics technicians normally complete a two-year program leading to an Associate of Science degree or an Associate of Applied Science degree.

COURSE REQUIREMENTS

Adhesives Technology
Compression and Injection
Dies and Molds
Drafting
Elastomers
Extrusion Processes
Introduction to Plastics

Materials Science
Molding Physics
Plastics Fabrication
Polymer Chemistry
Properties of Plastics
Reinforced Plastics
Strength of Materials

RECOMMENDED HIGH SCHOOL COURSES

Chemistry
Drafting
English

Industrial Arts
Mathematics (2 years or more)
Physics

CAREERS	D.O.T. NUMBERS	OUTLOOK	AVERAGE INITIAL SALARIES
Duplicator	754.684-038	Fair	$15,000
Fixture Builder	600.281-022	Good	19,600
Joint Maker	690.285-250	Fair	15,000
Molder	777.684-010	Fair	14,000
Toolmaker	601.281-026	Good	19,300

Occupational Personality Style: Technical

DPT Functions: Data = H   People = L   Things = H

GOE Work Groups: Craft Technology, Managerial Work: Mechanical

Plumbing

Plumbers install piping systems that carry steam, air, water, chemicals, and gases through structures. They may be self-employed contractors or work for other contractors.

EDUCATIONAL REQUIREMENTS

Some plumbers may complete a two-year program leading to an Associate of Science degree. Other plumbers may complete a training program lasting up to one year and receive a certificate of completion. Most plumbers are trained through a four-year apprenticeship. Most apprenticeship programs are administered by labor unions, labor guilds, or trade councils.

COURSE REQUIREMENTS

Algebra
Appliance Servicing
Brazing and Soldering
Fundamentals of Plumbing
Plumbing Codes and Ordinances

Plumbing Estimating
Plumbing Fixtures
Plumbing Practices
Working Drawings

RECOMMENDED HIGH SCHOOL COURSES

Drafting
English
Industrial Arts

Mathematics
Physics

The Career Connection for Technical Education

CAREERS	D.O.T. NUMBERS	OUTLOOK	AVERAGE INITIAL SALARIES
Pipe Fitter	862.261-022	Excellent	$32,600
Pipe Fitter Apprentice	862.381-026	Good	18,500
Plumber	862.381-030	Excellent	26,400
Plumber Apprentice	862.381-034	Fair	17,900
Plumber Supervisor	862.131-018	Fair	31,200
Plumbing Inspector	168.167-050	Fair	26,900

Occupational Personality Styles: Technical, Detail-oriented

DPT Functions: Data = H   People = L   Things = H

GOE Work Groups: Craft Technology, Production Work

Printing Technology

Printing technicians create type composition, do copy preparation, layout and design, paste-up, and phototypesetting. Printing technicians also do platemaking, presswork, and binding. Printing technicians may work as commercial printers, lithographers, platemakers, or paste-up artists. They usually work for newspaper and magazine publishers, advertising agencies, and commercial printing companies.

EDUCATIONAL REQUIREMENTS

Some printing technicians and illustrators may complete a two-year program leading to an Associate of Science degree. Many technicians and illustrators may develop expertise through apprenticeships and on-the-job training.

COURSE REQUIREMENTS

Engraving	Photography
Lithography	Printing Processes
Offset Presswork	Screen Printing
Paste-up	Typesetting

RECOMMENDED HIGH SCHOOL COURSES

Art	Printing Technology
Drafting	Psychology
English	Sociology
Fine Arts	

CAREERS	D.O.T. NUMBERS	OUTLOOK	AVERAGE INITIAL SALARIES
Engraver	979.381-010	Excellent	$30,000
Lithographic Platemaker	972.381-010	Excellent	28,200
Lithographic Platemaker Apprentice	972.381-014	Fair/Good	17,500
Offset Press Operator	651.382-042	Good	25,200
Paste-up Copy-camera Operator	979.381-022	Good	16,900
Photoengraver	971.381-022	Excellent	30,000
Photoengraver Apprentice	971.381-026	Excellent	20,500
Photoengraving Finisher	971.381-030	Good	24,000
Photoengraving Printer	971.381-034	Good	23,600

Occupational Personality Styles: Technical, Detail-oriented

DPT Functions: Data = H   People = L   Things = H

GOE Work Groups: Craft Technology, Production Work

Radiological Technology

Radiological technicians X-ray patients for therapeutic and diagnostic purposes. They operate specialized equipment and administer contrast agents orally or in enemas to make the patients' organs visible to that equipment.

EDUCATIONAL REQUIREMENTS

Radiological technicians normally complete a trade-school training program which may last up to one year and then receive a certificate of completion.

COURSE REQUIREMENTS

Anatomy
Medical Terminology
Microbiology
Photography
Physiology
Psychology

Radiation Protection
Radiographic Positioning
Radiologic Darkroom
   Techniques
Radiologic Technology

RECOMMENDED HIGH SCHOOL COURSES

Biology
Chemistry
English

Health
Mathematics

CAREERS	D.O.T. NUMBERS	OUTLOOK	AVERAGE INITIAL SALARIES
Radiologic Technologist	078.362-026	Excellent	$21,500
Radiologic Technologist, Chief	078.162-010	Excellent	28,900

Occupational Personality Styles: Technical, Detail-oriented

DPT Functions: Data = M   People = L   Things = H

GOE Work Groups: Craft Technology, Laboratory Technology

Real Estate

Real-estate agents appraise, buy, and sell land and buildings. They maintain a knowledge of current property values, show properties to clients, arrange for financing, and manage title transfers. Many real-estate agents manage rental and leasing properties. Real-estate agents work for real-estate broker agencies. Successful agents often obtain their brokerage licenses and open their own real-estate offices.

EDUCATIONAL REQUIREMENTS

Most states require a 100- to 200-hour training program for potential agents. In addition, they must pass a state licensing examination. Some agents complete a two-year program leading to an Associate of Science degree.

COURSE REQUIREMENTS

Accounting
Advertising
Business Law
Business Mathematics
Economics
Escrow Principles
Industrial and Commercial
   Real Estate
Marketing

Property Management
Real-Estate Appraisal
Real-Estate Financing
Real-Estate Investments
Real-Estate Laws
Real-Estate Principles
Retail Merchandising
Sales

RECOMMENDED HIGH SCHOOL COURSES

Accounting
Business
Business Law
Economics

English
Mathematics
Psychology
Typing/Word Processing

The Career Connection for Technical Education

CAREERS	D.O.T. NUMBERS	OUTLOOK	AVERAGE INITIAL SALARIES
Real Estate Agent	186.117-058	Good	$25,400
Real Estate Appraiser	191.267-010	Excellent	25,800
Real Estate Sales Representative	250.357-018	Good	25,000

Occupational Personality Styles: Influencing, Social

DPT Functions: Data = H   People = H   Things = L

GOE Work Groups: General Sales, Promotion, Sales Technology

Retailing and Marketing

Marketers work in a variety of fields. They may do marketing research, product testing, advertising, sales promotions, or direct sales. Employment opportunities may be found in advertising agencies, direct mail advertising, consumer product manufacturers, and phone advertising.

EDUCATIONAL REQUIREMENTS

Many marketers complete a two-year program leading to an Associate of Science degree or an Associate of Business Science degree. Some marketers gain on-the-job experience as phone solicitors and marketing surveyors.

COURSE REQUIREMENTS

Accounting
Advertising
Business Communications
Business Law
Cost Accounting
Data Processing
Economics
English
Human Relations

Marketing
Merchandising
Psychology
Public Speaking
Sales Management
Salesmanship
Small Business Management
Statistics

RECOMMENDED HIGH SCHOOL COURSES

Business
Economics
English

Mathematics
Psychology
Sociology

CAREERS	D.O.T. NUMBERS	OUTLOOK	AVERAGE INITIAL SALARIES
Buyer	162.157-018	Good/Exc.	$23,000
Buyer Assistant	162.157-022	Fair	17,000
Promotion Manager	163.117-018	Good	23,500
Purchasing Agent	162.157-038	Good	25,100
Retail Manager	185.167-046	Good/Exc.	23,000
Retail Store Manager	185.167-046	Excellent	23,000
Sales Manager	163.167-018	Excellent	24,100
Sales Representative		Good	22,800

Occupational Personality Styles: Social, Influencing

DPT Functions: Data = H   People = M   Things = L

GOE Work Groups: General Sales, Promotion, Sales Technology

Secretarial Science

Secretaries schedule appointments, screen telephone calls, and transcribe and type letters and documents. They coordinate special functions, take dictation, and greet visitors. Some secretaries may do general office work such as filing and copying as well. Some secretaries specialize as legal or medical secretaries. Word processing technicians use computerized word processing equipment to transcribe dictation and to produce, format, and revise correspondence and documents. Secretarial science employment opportunities exist in medical and legal offices, banks, insurance companies, businesses, and government agencies.

EDUCATIONAL REQUIREMENTS

Secretarial science professionals normally complete a two-year program leading to an Associate of Science degree, an Associate of Applied Science degree, or an Associate of Business Science degree.

COURSE REQUIREMENTS

Business Communications
Dictation

Office Procedures
Typing/Word Processing

Medical Secretary
Anatomy
Medical Ethics
Medical Office Management

Medical Terminology
Medical Transcription
Physiology

Legal Secretary
Business Law
Contracts

Legal Transcription
Legal Typing/Word Processing

Word Processing Technician
Automated Typing
Data Processing Principles
Information Management
    Systems

Information Processing
Word Processing

RECOMMENDED HIGH SCHOOL COURSES

Business Law
Business Machines Operations
Business Mathematics
Computer Operations

Data Processing
Dictation
English
Typing/Word Processing

CAREERS	D.O.T. NUMBERS	OUTLOOK	AVERAGE INITIAL SALARIES
Administrative Assistant	169.167-010	Excellent	$18,100
Administrative Secretary	169.167-014	Excellent	20,500
Clerical Secretary	201.362-030	Excellent	14,000
Legal Secretary	201.362-010	Excellent	16,500
Medical Secretary	079.367-018	Excellent	17,000
School Secretary	201.362-022	Poor	15,600
Social Secretary	201.162-010	Good	13,500

Occupational Personality Style: Detail-oriented

DPT Functions: Data = H   People = L   Things = L

GOE Work Groups: Administrative Detail, Clerical Machine Operation, Clerical Handling, Contracts and Claims

Surgical Technology

Surgical technicians assist surgeons in operating rooms. They prepare surgical equipment, instruments, operating-room lights, tables, and other equipment. They prepare patients for surgery and function as members of the surgical team by assisting with surgical procedures and providing instruments and other equipment to surgeons. Surgical technicians may find employment in hospitals and surgical clinics.

EDUCATIONAL REQUIREMENTS

Surgical technicians usually complete a trade-school program lasting up to one year. Some technicians gain experience in military hospitals.

COURSE REQUIREMENTS

Anatomy
Medical and Surgical
    Terminology
Microbiology
Operating Room Fundamentals
    (Surgical)
Pharmacology

Physiology
Sterilization Procedures
Surgical Instrument
    Identification
Surgical Procedures
Technician Orientation

RECOMMENDED HIGH SCHOOL COURSES

Biology
Chemistry
English

Health
Mathematics

CAREER	D.O.T. NUMBER	OUTLOOK	AVERAGE INITIAL SALARY
Surgical Technician	079.374-022	Excellent	$16,800

Occupational Personality Styles:	Scientific, Serving
DPT Functions:	Data = H People = M Things = H
GOE Work Groups:	Laboratory Technology, Medical Sciences

Surveying

Surveyors measure construction sites, help establish official land boundaries, and assist in setting land values. They collect information for maps and charts and use precise instruments to map the earth's contours, features, and boundaries. Some surveyors work as independent contractors. Most surveyors work for construction companies, engineering firms, or government agencies.

EDUCATIONAL REQUIREMENTS

Some surveyors complete trade-school training programs lasting several months and receive a certificate of completion. Many surveyors complete a two-year program leading to an Associate of Science degree. In most states, surveyors must be licensed and must show evidence of competence.

COURSE REQUIREMENTS

Botany
Cartography
Earth Science
Geology
Map Reading

Mathematics (including
   Trigonometry)
Surveying Techniques
Topography

RECOMMENDED HIGH SCHOOL COURSES

Botany
Drafting
Earth Science

English
Mathematics (including
   Trigonometry)

CAREERS	D.O.T. NUMBERS	OUTLOOK	AVERAGE INITIAL SALARIES
Geodetic Surveyor	018.167-038	Fair	$20,100
Land Surveyor	018.167-018	Fair	17,500
Marine Surveyor	018.167-046	Fair	21,600
Mine Surveyor	018.161-010	Fair	17,500
Surveyor Assistant	018.167-034	Fair	14,400

Occupational Personality Styles: Technical, Detail-oriented

DPT Functions: Data = H   People = L   Things = M

GOE Work Group: Engineering Technology

Telecommunications Technology

Telecommunications technicians may work in specialized areas of telecommunications. Aircraft electronics technicians install and maintain aircraft communications and navigations systems. Broadcast technicians operate and maintain television and radio transmission in accordance with FCC regulations. Telephone technicians install and maintain central and business telephone systems. Mobile-radio technicians install and service two-way radios, cellular telephone systems, and railroad traffic control systems. Satellite technicians install and maintain equipment used for sending and receiving satellite transmissions. Telecommunications employment opportunities exist with telephone companies, commercial broadcasting networks, radio and TV stations, telecommunication equipment manufacturers, and telecommunications equipment repairers.

EDUCATIONAL REQUIREMENTS

Most telecommunications technicians complete a two-year program leading to an Associate of Applied Science degree. Most jobs in this field require the successful completion of the FCC Radio/Telephone Licensing examination. In addition, technicians may also take the Certified Electronics Technician (CET) examination.

COURSE REQUIREMENTS

AC/DC Electricity
AC/DC Electronics
Antennas and Wave Propagation
Audio and RF Amplifiers
Digital and Data Communications
Electrical Power Distribution
Electromagnetics
Electronic Communications
Fiberoptic Communications

Microprocessor Theory
Microwave Communications
   Systems
Modulation Methods
Power Supplies
Resonant Circuits
Transmission Lines and Waveguides
Two-way Mobile Equipment
   Systems

RECOMMENDED HIGH SCHOOL COURSES

Drafting
Electrical Shop
English

Industrial Arts
Mathematics (3 years or more)
Physics

CAREERS	D.O.T. NUMBERS	OUTLOOK	AVERAGE INITIAL SALARIES
Cable Splicer	829.361-010	Good	$18,900
Cable Splicer Apprentice	829.361-014	Fair/Good	14,800
Communications Technician Supervisor	823.131-010	Good	24,000
Electronic Intelligence Operations Specialist	193.382-010	Good/Exc.	19,500
Line Installer Repairer	821.361-026	Excellent	18,900
Line Supervisor	821.131-014	Excellent	24,500
Radio Intelligence Operator	193.362-014	Good	17,000
Relay Technician	821.261-018	Good	18,200
Sound Technician	829.281-022	Good	18,200
Station Installer Repairer	822.261-022	Good	18,000
Telegraph Maintainer	822.381-022	Fair	17,500
Transmitter Operator	193.262-038	Good	17,900
Video Operator	194.282-010	Good/Exc.	18,300

Occupational Personality Styles: Technical, Detail-oriented

DPT Functions: Data = M   People = L   Things = H

GOE Work Group: Craft Technology

Tool and Die Design

Tool and die designers conceive and develop designs for machinery and equipment. They draw designs for various fixtures, jugs, and molds. They estimate costs and equipment life. They also estimate tools production materials. Most tool and die designers work for manufacturing companies or tool and die shops.

EDUCATIONAL REQUIREMENTS

Trade schools offer instruction lasting up to one year in tool and die design. However, many tool and die designers become apprentices in tool and die shops and receive considerable on-the-job training.

COURSE REQUIREMENTS

Algebra
Blueprint Reading
Design
Drafting
Materials Science

Metallurgy
Production Processes
Solid Geometry
Tool and Die Manufacturing

RECOMMENDED HIGH SCHOOL COURSES

Drafting
English
Industrial Arts

Mathematics (3 years or more)
Metal Shop
Physics

Travel and Tourism

Travel agents assist travelers in making travel plans, arranging trips for business and pleasure, and obtaining tickets and reservations. They conduct travel tours, do travel promotion and exhibits, and sell travel packages. Reservation clerks answer questions about fares and schedules and enter passenger data into computer terminals. Ticket agents handle passenger reservations and prepare tickets and boarding passes. Reservation clerks and ticket agents normally work for airlines, railway, and steamship companies. Travel agents work for travel agencies and may act as travel agency managers.

EDUCATIONAL REQUIREMENTS

Travel and tourism people are normally trained in schools owned by travel agencies. Training may last from a few weeks to several months. Some professionals may complete a two-year program leading to an Associate of Science degree or an Associate of Applied Science degree.

COURSE REQUIREMENTS

Accounting
English
Foreign Language
Geography
History
Marketing Sales
Mathematics

Office Skills
Psychology
Public Speaking
Sales Management
Tour Promotion
Travel and Transportation
Typing/Word Processing

RECOMMENDED HIGH SCHOOL COURSES

Business
Business Law
Computer Operations
English
Foreign Language

Geography
History
Mathematics
Speech
Typing/Word Processing

CAREERS	D.O.T. NUMBERS	OUTLOOK	AVERAGE INITIAL SALARIES
Tool and Die Apprentice	601.260-014	Good	$22,000
Tool and Die Maker	601.260-010	Excellent	26,500
Tool and Die Supervisor	601.130-010	Excellent	32,000
Tool Designer	007.061-026	Good	28,000
Tool Designer Apprentice	007.061-030	Good	22,000
Tool Drawing Checker	007.167-010	Good	24,200
Tool Planner	012.167-074	Good	26,800

Occupational Personality Styles: Technical, Detail-oriented

DPT Functions: Data = H   People = L   Things = H

GOE Work Groups: Craft Technology, Production Technology

Transportation Management

Transportation managers work in transportation, warehousing, and inventory management. They work with freight carriers, shipping companies, and freight warehousers. They interpret freight tariffs and Department of Transportation regulations. Transportation managers may work in sales, operations, and international business. Employment opportunities may be found in shipping companies; rail, trucking, and airline companies; package delivery companies; and industrial and manufacturing businesses.

EDUCATIONAL REQUIREMENTS

Transportation managers normally complete a two-year program leading to an Associate of Applied Science degree.

COURSE REQUIREMENTS

Accounting
Business Communications
Business Law
Carrier Management
Distribution Systems
Economics
English

Financial Mathematics
International Trade and
  Business
Marketing
Physical Distribution Management
Rates and Tariffs
Traffic Management

RECOMMENDED HIGH SCHOOL COURSES

Accounting
Business
Business Law
Computer Operations
Data Processing

English
Industrial Arts
Mathematics
Typing
Word Processing

CAREERS	D.O.T. NUMBERS	OUTLOOK
Transportation Agent	912.367-014	Excellent
Transportation Inspector	168.167-082	Excellent
Transportation Maintenance Supervisor	184.167-266	Good/Exc.

Occupational Personality Styles: Technical, Influencing

DPT Functions: Data = H   People = M   Th

GOE Work Groups: Business Administration, Qu trol

CAREERS	D.O.T. NUMBERS	OUTLOOK	AVERAGE INITIAL SALARIES
Tool and Die Apprentice	601.260-014	Good	$22,000
Tool and Die Maker	601.260-010	Excellent	26,500
Tool and Die Supervisor	601.130-010	Excellent	32,000
Tool Designer	007.061-026	Good	28,000
Tool Designer Apprentice	007.061-030	Good	22,000
Tool Drawing Checker	007.167-010	Good	24,200
Tool Planner	012.167-074	Good	26,800

Occupational Personality Styles: Technical, Detail-oriented

DPT Functions: Data = H   People = L   Things = H

GOE Work Groups: Craft Technology, Production Technology

Transportation Management

Transportation managers work in transportation, warehousing, and inventory management. They work with freight carriers, shipping companies, and freight warehousers. They interpret freight tariffs and Department of Transportation regulations. Transportation managers may work in sales, operations, and international business. Employment opportunities may be found in shipping companies; rail, trucking, and airline companies; package delivery companies; and industrial and manufacturing businesses.

EDUCATIONAL REQUIREMENTS

Transportation managers normally complete a two-year program leading to an Associate of Applied Science degree.

COURSE REQUIREMENTS

Accounting
Business Communications
Business Law
Carrier Management
Distribution Systems
Economics
English

Financial Mathematics
International Trade and
   Business
Marketing
Physical Distribution Management
Rates and Tariffs
Traffic Management

RECOMMENDED HIGH SCHOOL COURSES

Accounting
Business
Business Law
Computer Operations
Data Processing

English
Industrial Arts
Mathematics
Typing
Word Processing

CAREERS	D.O.T. NUMBERS	OUTLOOK	AVERAGE INITIAL SALARIES
Transportation Agent	912.367-014	Excellent	$19,500
Transportation Inspector	168.167-082	Excellent	23,100
Transportation Maintenance Supervisor	184.167-266	Good/Exc.	28,100

Occupational Personality Styles: Technical, Influencing

DPT Functions: Data = H   People = M   Things = M

GOE Work Groups: Business Administration, Quality Control

Travel and Tourism

Travel agents assist travelers in making travel plans, arranging trips for business and pleasure, and obtaining tickets and reservations. They conduct travel tours, do travel promotion and exhibits, and sell travel packages. Reservation clerks answer questions about fares and schedules and enter passenger data into computer terminals. Ticket agents handle passenger reservations and prepare tickets and boarding passes. Reservation clerks and ticket agents normally work for airlines, railway, and steamship companies. Travel agents work for travel agencies and may act as travel agency managers.

EDUCATIONAL REQUIREMENTS

Travel and tourism people are normally trained in schools owned by travel agencies. Training may last from a few weeks to several months. Some professionals may complete a two-year program leading to an Associate of Science degree or an Associate of Applied Science degree.

COURSE REQUIREMENTS

Accounting	Office Skills
English	Psychology
Foreign Language	Public Speaking
Geography	Sales Management
History	Tour Promotion
Marketing Sales	Travel and Transportation
Mathematics	Typing/Word Processing

RECOMMENDED HIGH SCHOOL COURSES

Business	Geography
Business Law	History
Computer Operations	Mathematics
English	Speech
Foreign Language	Typing/Word Processing

CAREERS	D.O.T. NUMBERS	OUTLOOK	AVERAGE INITIAL SALARIES
Tourist Information Assistant	237.167-014	Fair	$14,100
Travel Agent	252.152-010	Fair	17,200
Travel Clerk	238.362-014	Good	12,900
Travel Counselor	238.167-014	Fair	17,200

Occupational Personality Styles: Serving, Social

DPT Functions: Data = H   People = H   Things = L

GOE Work Groups: Administrative Detail, General Sales, Hospitality Services

Truck Driving

Truck drivers haul cargo over long and short distances. They check the condition of the truck before and while traveling and may perform maintenance as needed. Truck drivers ensure that trucks are properly loaded and balanced and that Department of Transportation (DOT) regulations are met. Many truck drivers work for trucking companies or industrial companies. Some truck drivers are owner-operators of their own cab and/or trailer and do contract work.

EDUCATIONAL REQUIREMENTS

Truck drivers must have a chauffeur's license for the class of vehicle they are driving. This license is obtained after passing written and road tests in the presence of state examiners. Some truck drivers complete training programs at truck driving schools which lead to a certificate of completion.

COURSE REQUIREMENTS

Defensive Driving
Diesel Engine Theory
DOT Rules and Regulations
Driving Skills

Road Safety
Truck Maintenance
Weight Distribution

RECOMMENDED HIGH SCHOOL COURSES

Auto Shop
Business
Driver Education

English
Mathematics

CAREERS	D.O.T. NUMBERS	OUTLOOK	AVERAGE INITIAL SALARIES
Truck Driver, Heavy	905.663-014	Excellent	$27,800
Truck Driver, Light	906.683-022	Excellent	21,800

Occupational Personality Styles: Technical, Detail-oriented

DPT Functions: Data = L   People = L   Things = H

GOE Work Group: Land and Water Vehicle Operation

Welding Technology

Welders follow blueprints to cut, fabricate, weld, and braze metals together. They may operate sheers, rolls, drills, and brakes to fabricate parts. They may operate hoists and cranes to handle heavy objects. Welders also repair broken and worn metal parts using welding, brazing, or soft soldering techniques. Welders may be employed as iron workers, pipe fitters, or boiler makers. Employment opportunities are generally found within the construction industry.

EDUCATIONAL REQUIREMENTS

Welders may complete programs which last for several months at trade schools. Some welders may complete a two-year program leading to an Associate of Science degree or an Associate of Applied Science degree. Apprenticeship programs are administered by labor unions and trade councils which supply training to welders.

COURSE REQUIREMENTS

Acetylene Cutting
Arc Welding
Basic Electricity
Blueprint Reading
Drafting
Fabrication and Layout
Heat Treatment
Hydraulics

Manufacturing Processes
Metallurgy
MIG/TIG Welding
Nondestructive Testing
Oxyacetylene Welding
Pneumatics
Technical Mathematics
Welding and Brazing

RECOMMENDED HIGH SCHOOL COURSES

Drafting
English
Industrial Arts

Mathematics
Metal Shop

CAREERS	D.O.T. NUMBERS	OUTLOOK	AVERAGE INITIAL SALARIES
Arc Welder	810.384-014	Excellent	$21,100
Experimental Welder	819.281-022	Excellent	24,100
Welder Apprentice	810.384-010	Good	15,100
Welder Fitter	819.361-010	Good	19,000

Occupational Personality Styles: Technical, Detail-oriented

DPT Functions: Data = H   People = L   Things = H

GOE Work Groups: Craft Technology, Production Work

Auxiliary Information

There is a definite relationship between the type and level of education one pursues and career choices. When one makes plans for education or careers it is more helpful to begin with the end in mind. The following questions may be important to ask:

1. What career do I want?
2. Will the job that I want today be the one I want 20 years from now?
3. How far do I want to go in education or training?
4. What type of education or training will I be happiest in pursuing?
5. Will my intended educational plans help me get the job I want?
6. If I begin my education along one path and change, what effect will it have?

As you study the alternatives on the accompanying chart, remember these important points:

1. There are several ways to become trained and educated.
2. There are several careers available in each occupational field.
3. To enter certain jobs, you must have certain levels of education.
4. Generally speaking, the more training or education you have, the higher the number of available jobs.
5. You can change your mind about the level or type of training, but it is easier and less time-consuming to begin on the right track.

ALTERNATIVES FOR POST-HIGH SCHOOL EDUCATION

Specialized School

Short-term (6 to 24 months), specialized training in a technical area is provided by this type of school. Very few "non-essential" classes are required. Quite often a technical school provides only one area of emphasis, such as dental technology, cosmetology, business, etc.

Technical College

Here, general education courses are mixed with technical training. A technical college may offer associate degrees that transfer to a four-year college or university. More often, programs are terminal in nature, preparing students for careers upon completion.

Two-year Community College

These are also called junior colleges. While short-term degrees are offered, most students attend these schools in preparation for four-year colleges or universities. You can earn an associate degree in two years or transfer any time after the first enrollment.

Four-year College

An associate degree or bachelor degree can be earned at this level of higher education. Some four-year colleges also offer limited graduate degrees. A wide variety of courses is available.

University

A university provides a great variety of course work and several levels of degrees. A university is divided into several "colleges," such as the College of Business or the College of Biological Sciences. Degrees range from associate, bachelor, master, and doctoral programs. Each college is composed of several departments. A department may offer one or more majors.

Transfer of Credit

Students often accumulate credit at one school then transfer to another one in order to complete a degree. If courses are college-level courses, the credit will transfer from one accredited institution to another. When a student transfers to a new school, official transcripts of all credits must be sent from all previous institutions to the admissions office of the new institution.

GRADUATION REQUIREMENTS

Credit Hour

Credit is awarded for courses based on the amount of time spent in class per week. For example, a five-credit course generally requires one to be in class five periods each week. A two-hour class requires two class periods per week. Often a laboratory period is extra at a technical school or a technical college. An average load is 14–17 quarter or semester hours for each registration.

Quarter Hour

In a quarter system, the year is divided into four parts. One academic year equals three quarters.

Semester Hour

There are three semesters in one year. One academic year equals two semesters.

Transfer

When you transfer from a quarter system to a semester system it may appear that you lose credits. Just remember that there are three quarters but only two semesters in each academic year. Therefore, three quarter hours credit equals two semester hours credit.

Graduation

This denotes an academic accomplishment that has been outlined by the school. Basic requirements usually include:

1. general education courses
2. courses in a major field of study
3. a minimum number of credit hours
4. passing specifically required examinations or courses

Degrees

Various degrees are awarded by schools. The first three are usually obtained at technical schools, technical colleges, or specialty schools.

Types of Degrees

1. **Certificate:** a six- to twelve-month course
2. **Junior college degree:** a one-year course
3. **Associate degree of Applied Science or Arts:** a two-year degree that usually does not transfer all credits to a college or university
4. **Associate of Arts or Science:** a two-year degree used for job preparation or transferring
5. **Bachelor of Arts or Science:** a four-year degree
6. **Master of Arts or Science, Engineering, Business, etc.:** a one- to two-year course beyond the bachelor level
7. **Doctor of Education, Philosophy, Medicine, etc.:** a two- to four-year course beyond the master level

General Education

Breadth of knowledge is at least as important as depth of knowledge. To ensure that students are well educated, technical schools require students to take a number of classes in a variety of areas.

Major

When a student decides the specialty desired, a major is selected. The courses are usually sequential, starting with the simple and moving to the more complex.

Getting admitted to a college of your choice takes time and effective planning. Often, what you have accomplished as early as the ninth grade will impact your chances for admissions. The closer you get to graduation, the more important it will become to know clearly the steps that will help. Your counselors are an indispensable part of your admissions efforts. They are in contact with college representatives and have both experience and information that will be helpful. Below is a sequence that can become meaningful to you. It is followed by a description of each step.

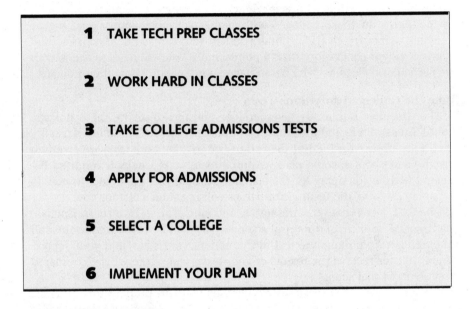

1   TAKE TECH PREP CLASSES

2   WORK HARD IN CLASSES

3   TAKE COLLEGE ADMISSIONS TESTS

4   APPLY FOR ADMISSIONS

5   SELECT A COLLEGE

6   IMPLEMENT YOUR PLAN

Take Tech Prep Classes

Beginning with the ninth grade, the specific high school courses that you choose will be important in your admission to college. Technical and vocational colleges, especially those that cannot accept all the applicants that apply, have outlined specific courses that are designated *tech prep*. A rule of thumb is that if a class is both required for graduation and is a technically oriented course, it is considered tech prep. Examples would be drafting, graphic arts, industrial arts, and welding.

Selective vocational colleges and technical institutes request that from 50% to 70% of your classes in high school be tech prep. Avoid the reasoning that you will build your grades by taking non-tech prep courses. On the other hand, look for the opportunity to take honors and especially advanced placement courses. How serious a student is about higher education is often reflected in the types of classes taken.

Work Hard in the Classes

Grades and grade point averages are calculated, for admissions decisions, from the ninth through the twelfth grades. Typically an "A" = 4 points, "B" = 3 points, "C" = 2 points, and "D" = 1 point. You can calculate your cumulative grade point average by (1) multiplying the units (for example, hours) of each class times the points earned for the grade of the class—this is called the grade point, (2) add up the total units for all the classes, (3) add the grade points for all the classes, and (4) divide the total grade points by the total number of units.

Most colleges look at the total or cumulative grade point average (GPA) for all your classes. However, there are some colleges and universities that are highly selective that also want the GPA for tech prep courses. Although not common, in these colleges with highly selective admissions, higher weighted points are given for honors and advanced placement courses (that is, an "A" might equal more than 4 points, etc.). You will need to check with the particular college for which you have an interest to know their policies.

Take the College Admissions Tests

The two most frequently given college entrance tests are the Scholastic Aptitude Test (SAT) and the American College Test (ACT). Colleges usually have a preference for the test they want you to take. Both tests are given on specific dates at a specific place. Approximately six weeks is required between the time you apply for the test and the date you will take it. If you do not apply on time, the testing companies will not send a test for you.

The SAT has verbal and numerical sections. The ACT tests in English, math, social science, and natural science. You will be compared against all other students who take the test in the nation, your state, and your school. When colleges receive the results of your tests, your score will be compared to students in that school.

A large controversy exists as to whether you can prepare for the tests. Studies have resulted in conflicting findings. It is, however, to your advantage to become familiar with the types of questions you will be encountering on the tests. Your counselor will be able to help you with booklets provided from the testing company.

Apply for Admissions

Before applying for admission to a college, find out about their admissions policies. For example, there are three types of admissions. Colleges with an *open* admissions policy require a high school diploma or its equivalent and typically have a minimum age factor. Many colleges have a *selective* admissions policy, which requires specific information such as GPA and college entrance examination scores. These colleges have established minimum requirements regarding grades and test results that are necessary for a student to attain. A third category includes those colleges (typically large universities that have graduate programs and conduct research) that have a *highly selective* policy for admissions. They also require GPA and test scores, but they often require other information such as percent of your high school courses that are college prep, GPA on your college prep courses, letters of recommendation, an essay from you to identify your educational goals and to test your writing ability, interviews, and a record of extra-curricular activities. If the college is sponsored by a church, an endorsement from your ecclesiastical leader may be requested.

When letters of recommendation are requested, understand that the college is interested in knowing how well you can do academically. Therefore, avoid the temptation of having a friend, community leader, or neighbor write a letter elaborating on other than educational endeavors. Those letters that have the most influence are from teachers of strong academic courses.

Students are sometimes disappointed when they fail to get their application completed and to the college before the deadline. Most colleges have deadlines, and those with selective or highly selective admissions policies hold strictly to that deadline.

Your counselor typically has copies of catalogs of local institutions and those where many of the students in your school have traditionally enrolled. If they are not readily available, the counselor can help you find where to write for catalogs and application materials.

Select a College

When selecting a college there are several factors to consider. One of the first is finances. Limited finances may suggest that you attend a college while living at home. Costs of housing and food are often expensive. The cost of tuition also influences finances. Work with your counselor to identify all the costs that you will incur at the colleges you are considering. Compare the costs to your financial resources.

Another important factor to consider is whether the college has the academic major that you want to study. If you have not chosen a major, this may not be a significant determinant. However, if you are considering a major such as nursing or engineering, it is important to begin at the college from which you want to graduate. The reason is that courses in these programs are highly sequential and begin the first semester that you enroll. If you miss the first sequence, you may have to wait a complete year for the sequence to begin again. Because the number of majors that are very structured is increasing, it is usually a good practice to start at the school from which you want to get your degree.

If you plan to attend a community college in order to take your general education courses and then transfer to a four-year college or university, select your courses carefully. While all college-level courses transfer from one accredited institution to another, they may not fit into the category you intended. For example, a class that is considered a general education course in physical science at a community college may not be classified as the same in a particular four-year college. It will transfer as an elective, but not in the area you intended. The same is also true for classes in one's major. Most community colleges have lists of their courses and how they transfer to specific local institutions. Acquire those lists and select your courses with your transfer in mind.

Other considerations are important in selecting a college. A few are distance from home, size of the student body, athletic or fine arts programs, and work opportunities. Take time and carefully consider your choice. College is costly in both time and money.

Implement Your Plan

The time between your application for admissions and when you go to school is important. Here are a few things to consider.

When you apply for admission, the application will usually ask for the major you intend to pursue. Even if you are not certain, select a major that you are considering and list it. Most colleges will send you valuable information about that particular major, which will include the courses they recommend for your first enrollment period.

Check on housing and make the necessary arrangements early to increase the probability of getting a desired roommate or living in an area of your liking. If a job is necessary for you, find out how to apply for on-campus jobs and locate off-campus possibilities; begin aggressively pursuing potential opportunities. Contact the financial aid office early and continue this association until you are satisfied that you have your financial aids package firmly in place.

THE ANATOMY OF A JOB

There are many aspects of a particular job that are important to consider when making career choices. Following is a brief outline of the major components. Remember that decisions are enhanced or inhibited by the accuracy of the information and perception you have about a particular job. One of the most helpful steps in making your decisions is to fantasize yourself in the job—working in the environment, doing the tasks, and being with the people. Ask yourself when doing this very productive daydreaming: "Am I comfortable in this situation? Can I do what is necessary?"

Working Conditions

Based on periodic job analysis, these may change from place to place and as different phenomenon occur.

1. Indoor/outdoor work environment
2. Indoor temperature changes and ranges
3. Humidity ranges and changes
4. Noise and vibration
5. Hazards
6. Fumes, odors, toxic conditions, dust, and ventilation

Tasks or Duties

Not only are the specific tasks important to know, but the types of tasks offer you the opportunity to express yourself.

1. Working primarily with data, people, or things
2. The relationship of work with these three elements

General Nature and Description

This component is strongly related to the type of lifestyle you can live as a result of your particular job.

1. Hours—shift or regular
2. Physical or mental exertion
3. Flexible, creative, or routine work
4. Individual or teamwork atmosphere
5. Work for self or supervisor
6. Salaried or time card
7. Travel or stationary
8. Extracurricular requirements

Places of Employment

Geography is often one of the single most influential factors in a career choice. People will often compromise other factors to live in a particular area.

1. Size of organization
2. Location—urban/rural
3. Organizational structure
4. Public/private

Outlook

Outlook refers to both the availability of jobs at job entry and the longevity of that job and related horizontal or lateral opportunities.

Entry:	Longevity:
Availability	Opportunities for advancement
Competition	Projected forecast of industry
Locations	turnover rate
Obligations	Physical considerations—
Union memberships	Pregnancy
	Additional training needs
	Tenure date

Salary and Benefits

While the initial salary is important, perhaps a greater impact on your financial life will be the projected increases. These future increases are more dependent on the amount of education you have than initial salaries.

1. Entry level
2. Rate-of-inflation increases
3. Mode of payment—overtime, salary, piecework, or commission
4. Projected ceilings
5. Bonuses
6. Rate-of-pay increases
7. Medical benefits
8. Profit sharing
9. Stock options
10. Educational benefits
11. Travel
12. Discounts
13. Physical fitness opportunities
14. Retirement
15. Housing
16. Cost-of-living adjustments
17. Child care
18. Union benefits

Indexes

Index of Majors

The Career Connection for Technical Education

Index of Careers

Supervisor, numerous
Supervisory medical technologist, 115
Surgical technician, 139
Surveyor
  assistant, 141
  geodetic, 141
  land, 141
  marine, 141
  mine, 141

Technical writer, 99
Technician, numerous
Technologist, numerous
Telegraph maintainer, 143
Telephone maintenance
  mechanic, 65
Terminal operator, 93
Test technician, 71
Tester
  diesel engine, 57
  food products, 59
  water quality, 73
Tissue technologist, 115
Tool and die apprentice, 145
Tool and die maker, 145
Tool and die supervisor, 145
Tool design drafter, 61
Tool designer, 107, 145
Tool designer apprentice, 107, 145
Tool drawing checker, 145
Tool planner, 145
Tool setter, 105
Toolmaker, 125
Tourist information assistant, 149

Tractor mechanic, 25
Transcribing machine operator, 93
Transmission engineer, 33
Transmitter operator, 143
Transportation agent, 147
Transportation inspector, 147
Transportation maintenance
  supervisor, 147
Travel agent, 149
Travel clerk, 149
Travel counselor, 149
Truck driver, heavy, 151
Truck driver, light, 151
Tune-up mechanic, 25
Typist, 93
  data, 93

Vegetable farmer, 75
Video engineer, 33
Video operator, 143
Videotape recording engineer, 33
Vine crop farmer, 75

Water quality tester, 73
Waxer, dental, 55
Welder appentice, 153
Welder, arc, 153
Welder, experimental, 153
Welder fitter, 153
Wirer, electrician, 63
Wood machinist, 37
Wood patternmaker, 37
Word processing supervisor, 93
Writer, technical, 99

The Career Connection for Technical Education

OCCUPATIONAL OUTLOOK HANDBOOK
1994-1995 Edition — *By U.S. Department of Labor*

This low-cost JIST edition of the U.S. Department of labor's popular career exploration guide describes the 250 jobs in which 85% of the American workforce is employed. Valuable information about each occupation includes a description of the work itself, employment outlook and opportunities, earnings, related occupations, training and advancement, and sources of additional information.

OTHER INFORMATION

- THE standard career reference book
- The most widely used and known career reference for professionals and schools
- Includes the latest Department of Labor statistics

8-1/2 x 11, Paper, 473 pp. ISBN 1-56370-160-X **$15.95** *Order Code OOH4*	8-1/2 x 11, Hardback, 473 pp. ISBN 1-56370-161-8 **$21.95** *Order Code OOHH4*

AMERICA'S TOP JOBS MULTIMEDIA

A Multimedia Computer Program Providing Information on Over 250 Jobs

This computer software integrates text, sound, voice, and still full-color images featuring information found in the *Occupational Outlook Handbook*. Careful attention has been given to make this software easy to use--so easy, we think that it is even fun! Search for occupations in a number of ways including earnings, educational requirements, and employment.

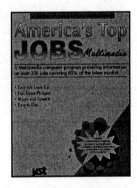

ISBN 1-56370-113-8 **3 1/2 Disk** *Order Code ATJM3* **$295.00**	ISBN 1-56370-115-4 **5 1/4 Disk** *Order Code ATJM5* **$295.00**	ISBN 1-56370-167-7 **CD Rom** *Order Code ATJMCD* **$295.00**

---

*Look for these and other fine books from **JIST Works, Inc.**, at your full service bookstore or call us for additional information at 800-648-5478.*

DICTIONARY OF OCCUPATIONAL TITLES
Revised Fourth Edition

This is THE definitive career reference book compiled by the U.S. Department of Labor. The DOT's classification system is THE standard for describing jobs. Each job code reveals the level of skills required to work with people, data, and things, and each job description includes detailed occupational information. It's organized by major job categories and cross-referenced by industry and job title.

ISBN 1-56370-006-9	ISBN 1-56370-000-X
Hardback 1 Vol.	**Paper 2 Vol.**
Order Code: DOTH	*Order Code: DOT91*
$48.00	**$39.00**

THE COMPLETE GUIDE FOR OCCUPATIONAL
EXPLORATION — *By JIST Editorial Staff*

First revision since 1984! Based on the new *Dictionary of Occupational Titles, The Complete Guide* contains up-to-date information on today's occupations, many of which have been created or greatly changed by technology. More than 12,000 occupations are organized into:

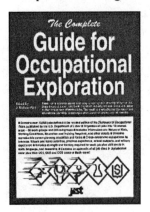

- 12 major interests areas
- 66 work groups
- 348 subgroups of related jobs

Includes an alphabetical appendix listing almost 30,000 jobs.

OTHER INFORMATION
- A must book for career counselors, professionals, and school personnel
- The only book of its kind with up-to-date information
- One of the three major reference books used by job placement counselors

8-1/2 x 11, Paper, 936 pp.	8-1/2 x 11, Hardback, 936 pp.
ISBN 1-56370-052-2	ISBN 1-56370-100-6
Order Code CGOE	*Order Code CGOEH*
$34.95	**$44.95**

---

*Look for these and other fine books from **JIST Works, Inc.**, at your full service bookstore or call us for additional information at 800-648-5478.*

HIRE LEARNING—Your Guide to a Successful School-to-Work
Transition — *Newly Revised! A Complete Three-Book Curriculum!*
Developed by Patricia Duffy and Walter Wannie

This is a complete and major revision of the widely acclaimed curriculum. *Hire Learning* has been field tested with thousands of students and reinforces the importance of basic academic skills and responsible behavior to prepare students for a successful transition from school to work. The three-book set includes both interesting text and activities—everything needed to present the material in a class or individual setting.
Instructor's Guide also available.

Setting Your Career and Life Direction ISBN 1-56370-188-X 8-1/2 x 11, Paper, 112 pp. *Order Code J188X* **$8.95**	**Landing a Job** ISBN 1-56370-189-8 8-1/2 x 11, Paper, 112 pp. *Order Code J1898* **$8.95**	**Succeeding in Your Work and Community** ISBN 1-56370-190-1 8-1/2 x 11, Paper, 112 pp. *Order Code J1901* **$8.95**

GETTING THE JOB YOU REALLY WANT 2nd Edition
A Step-by-Step Guide
by J. Michael Farr

This intensive career planning and job search workbook helps readers clarify what they want in a job and provides specific information on more than 200 careers. Those who know what kind of job they want will find help in identifying the skills to emphasize in interviews and information on relationed jobs.

OTHER INFORMATION:

- Easy to read and use
- Includes activities, examples, and checklists
- Techniques to cut job search time in half

8-1/2 x 11, Paper, 148 pp. ISBN 1-56370-092-1 *Order Code RWR* **$9.95**

---

*Look for these and other fine books from **JIST Works, Inc.**, at your full service bookstore or call us for additional information at 800-648-5478.*

AMERICA'S TOP JOBS FOR COLLEGE GRADUATES

Detailed Information on Jobs and Trends for College Grads — and Those Considering a College Education
by U.S. Department of Labor and J. Michael Farr

Nearly 2 million graduates enter or reenter the job market each year. This newest addition to JIST's America's series explains why college graduates can expect to make more money and defines the latest labor market and career planning trends through the year 2005. Also includes information on the 500 most popular jobs, and details on employment trends by major industry.

OTHER INFORMATION:

- Comprehensive appendices
- Based on the most current information from the Department of Labor
- Special section on job search and career planning

8-1/2 x 11, Paper, 300 pp.
ISBN 1-56370-140-5
Order Code ATCG
$14.95

AMERICA'S TOP TECHNICAL AND TRADE JOBS

Good Jobs That Don's Require Four Years of College
Edited and Compiled by J. Michael Farr

Like the other books in this series, this book provides job descriptions for more than 50 of the top technical and trade jobs in the U.S. economy. As many as 80 percent of the new jobs created do not require a college degree but do require technical skills! Determine which skills to upgrade to remain competitive in the work force and move up in your career.

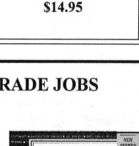

OTHER INFORMATION:

- Over 50 detailed job descriptions
- Other solid data on 300 jobs
- Special section on job search and career planning

8-1/2 x 11, Paper, 232 pp.
ISBN 1-56370-116-2
Order Code ATT
$11.95

---

*Look for these and other fine books from **JIST Works, Inc.**, at your full service bookstore or call us for additional information at 800-648-5478.*

THE QUICK RESUME and COVER LETTER BOOK —
Write and Use an Effective Resume in Only One Day
By J. Michael Farr

First title in JIST's new Quick Guides series, by a best-selling author whose job search books have sold more than one million copies! Contains an "Instant Resume Worksheet" that enables job seekers to put together a basic, acceptable resume in less than one day. Provides helpful advice on creating job objectives, identifying skills, dealing with special situations, and getting a job.

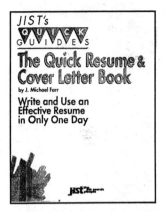

OTHER INFORMATION:

- Logical structure makes information easy to locate
- Contains more than 50 sample resumes and cover letters
- Crucial career planning and job search sections

> 7 x 9, Paper, 288 pp.
> ISBN 1-56370-141-3
> *Order Code RCLQG*
> **$9.95**

JOB SAVVY — *How To Be a Success at Work*
by LaVerne Ludden Ed.D.

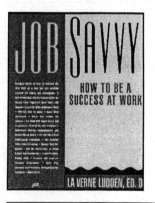

This book was written to help new employees learn the basics of successful job behavior such as good attendance, punctuality, and reliability. Job Savvy focuses on developing workplace skills that pay off—skills that get results that can get you noticed. Too many people learn the hard way about what it takes to get ahead on a job. Get a jump start on your successful career after reading this book!

OTHER INFORMATION:

- Separate Instructor's Guide
- Many exercises, forms, and worksheets
- Thorough, practical advice

> 8-1/2 x 11, Paper, 169 pp.
> ISBN 0-942784-79-0
> *Order Code JS*
> **$10.95**

---

*Look for these and other fine books from **JIST Works, Inc.**, at your full service bookstore or call us for additional information at 800-648-5478.*

jist the

JIST Works, Inc.
h Park Avenue
s, IN 46202-3431

JIS   se consider ordering
one or n   .

Or   itional copies of this
or other   Our offices are open
weekda

QTY			TOTAL
		rsion 5	
		on e	
		e 5	
		ical .95	
		4.95	
		50-X	
		y	
	DEMCO		

	The Very Quick Job Search: *Get a Good Job in Less Time* • ISBN 1-56370-181-2 • **$12.95**	
	The Resume Solution: *How to Write and Use a Resume That Gets Results* • ISBN 1-56370-180-4 • **$9.95**	
	Dictionary of Occupational Titles: *2-Volume Set* • ISBN 1-56370-000-X • **$39.00**	